1981

Cults and Cons

The Exploitation of the Emotional Growth Consumer

Cults and Cons

The Exploitation of the Emotional Growth Consumer

**Kenneth Cinnamon &
Dave Farson**

Nelson-Hall nh *Chicago*

Library of Congress Cataloging in Publication Data

Cinnamon, Kenneth M
    Cults and cons.
      1. Self-actualization (Psychology) 2. Group
relations training. I. Farson, Dave, joint
author. II. Title.
BF637.S4C56   158   79-1174
ISBN 0-88229-456-3 (cloth)
ISBN 0-88229-671-x (paper)

Manufactured in the United States of America

10   9   8   7   6   5   4   3   2   1

Contents

Foreword

Drs. Cinnamon and Farson have provided us with a fast paced, fun-loving, serious assault on the fusillade of human potential prophets and programs and "new" psychotherapies. This book is long overdue. The authors give no sympathy and ask for no sympathy. They point out the nonsense in the promise that "If you become dependent on us you will become a free-choosing, independent person." They show the reader the parallels of primitive cultism and the practices in the Emotional Growth Movement. If the reader wants to become a better human potential and psychotherapy consumer, this book can help tremendously. Well-meaning mental health professionals and volunteers can help themselves and their consumers by absorbing the main points that Cinnamon and Farson state so incisively.

For the last several years there has been an onslaught of self-help books and human potential growth groups, programs, and centers. All of these have attacked the unwitting but eager and, perhaps, confused public. The confusion and complexities of our expanded world, cities, and budgets left many of us feeling as if we had reached our levels of incompetence in work, fun, and love. And maybe it wasn't just a feeling.

The reading public has, in turn, responded by making many self-help books best sellers— eagerly gulping in practically anything that seemed to help it feel good in feeling inadequate. It has been fed an old diet repackaged and with new reasoning added. The message is rather consistent. Get "in touch" with your self-defeating patterns; feel bad; remember the cause is in your ego state, unfulfilled love, needs, and your fear of self-disclosure and taking risks; get through these obstacles to self-realization and there is the psychic bonanza of fulfillment awaiting you at the end of your journey.

Emotional Growth Groups and "new" psychotherapies have exploded into the scene hand in hand with the self-help books. It is frightening that practically none of these approaches has basis in research. They were not so new to be justified as something creative and fresh. There are not even historical allies in the evolution of human progress to give significant credence to the main thrust of these movements and therapies.

We human beings have progressed by developing better ways of meeting the challenges we confront. We have not progressed by giving a great deal of attention to the errors of our ways other than acknowledging ineffectiveness when it happens. In achieving personal satisfactions in today's world of love, work, play, and learning, the same principle holds. We are much more likely to gain satisfactions when we learn how to rather than how not to, or how we can instead of why we didn't. It is much more effective and enriching to learn how we can think for ourselves than to spend time with why we can't. It is much more fun to learn to be playful and develop a sense of humor than try to find out why we take things too seriously. It is much more satisfying and exciting to learn how to love than it is to go through the long tenuous journey of why we don't in order, as the dogma preaches, to remove the obstacles within us.

We have added to our search for the love of God. We are turning to our fellow human beings seeking ways to be loved. The authors have pointed to the ways in which the Emotional Growth Movement is furthering this quest to be loved instead of learning ways to be more loving through knowledge, reason, attentiveness, empathy, and practice.

Jan B. Roosa, Ph.D.
Gestalt and Social Competence Institute
Shawnee Mission, Kansas

Acknowledgments

Our special thanks to the following individuals for their assistance and support: Helen Shea and Sue Paduch for their diligent typing and proofreading; Allen Cinnamon and Sandy Kimball for their insight, consultation and contributions; our families and friends for their patience and understanding; and to you, the consumer, for your willingness to take a second look.

Introduction

What is life all about?
What is my place in it?
Who am I, and why am I hurting?

Life is sometimes a kick in the teeth, a shaft of darkness surrounded by great light. It is realistic to see life as a gesticulating, writhing monster, which is filled with paradox—pity and power, ice and fire. Is it unrealistic to expect compassion or empathy from such a creature? Is it possible to find moments of peace, hours of happiness in the spaces between those flick-flick movements of writhing pain and suffering?

It is not sophomoric to ask such questions. We embark on a journey of exploration. And, ultimately, our travels lead to self-explanation.

As we move against the sometimes monstrous confines of life, we seek help and reassurance. We look for something which will spread light in our darkness, which will make bearable that writhing pain called life. We seek warmth amid cold. We seek coolness under the sun. We are afraid and we do not wish to face the monster alone.

Some of us invent God. Others have sought many gods. Still others, unable to bear the weight of questions, search for answers in pills, bottles, on television, or wherever lies ground fertile enough for the growth of gods.

We live in an age of psychology. We live in a time when those gods which control the lives of men have come down from the mountain tops, have left their bushes and snakes and rivers. Our anxieties and fears have become civilized and sophisticated.

All of this required time. Then God, with a capital "G" and now singular in number and definite in gender, left those monuments called churches to his faithful few and went out into the land looking for therapeutic ways in which to respond to the fears of his flock.

God and man found psychology.

Now the psychiatrist has become the priest, the clinical psychologist the witch doctor. The litany of prayer has become the language of therapy. From hands and knees we have moved to couch or chair. The weekly service is still the appointed hour. And none of this is bad. It was inevitable. As the church became more institutionalized in its heroic attempt to live in both the past and the future, to respond to the whole person, to provide broad answers to very specific, personal questions, its defeat was certain.

We found psychology because as we took over the responsibility for our lives, we needed help in carrying the weight. We are heavy unto ourselves. And God found psychology because, relieved of our burden, he was trying to help.

Self is the new god. "I" is king—with both the power and responsibility of such a role. We are supposed to know the answers, know how to cope, know how to get along. Where before we asked God "why" when He allowed things to go wrong for us, we, alone, are now the bottom line. Or, we have believed those who would make us the causes of our worlds. Do we really have both freedom and power enough to control our lives? Do we really want to play God? This transition from sin to self holds implications important to our very psychological survival. To invent ourselves as God may be the most cruel of ironies. To become the inventor of God may be a role too heavy to bear.

This movement from pagan ritual to church litany to the therapeutic session is not to be lamented. It was and is a natural progression. And diverse has long been an adjective for the noun man. We have sought answers to the questions of living from many sources. Throughout our history we have expected much from our gods. We expected and do expect much from our God. Now our expectations of psychology are high. This is a natural and dangerous process. Perhaps from God we have asked too much.

However, it is not with our demands per se that we are now concerned. At this point, we are afraid of what psychology is supplying. Psychology, like God, sometimes works in strange, and not always wonderous ways. And the believers, like the true ones of the past, are sometimes caught in the trap of their own expectations and assumptions. Therefore, this book does not claim to be a new Bible, rather its message is: Beware the many Bibles!

Today there is a movement sweeping across the plains of our psychological landscape. The Human Potential Movement or Emotional Growth Movement, as religion of old, claims to have the answer for the questions of the multitude. And perhaps it does contain much good.

Yet, it is now time to examine this "new religion," to focus on its assumptions and offerings with the microscope of reality. Yes, God may work in wonderous ways, but men sometimes make that work strange. Religion became church, but what now has psychology become?

The Human Potential Movement or Emotional Growth Movement is an umbrella concept used to protect and encompass many different kinds of therapeutic techniques and offerings. There are group and individual therapies, mental and physical techniques, and various combinations of each, whose purposes purport to be the enhancement of psychological growth within the person and the breakdown of barriers between people. These are admirable goals and are to be applauded. However, it is our contention that the umbrella of "growth" has opened too wide to protect or encompass too many nontherapeutic pitches. Now it is time to separate the high priest from the low con. Now it is time to examine the assumptions of the growth movement, its techniques and goals and to ask:

What hath man wrought?
What kind of god is this?

The authors, functioning as teachers and counselors, have seen too many people injured by life and the Band-Aids supplied by various techniques or movements. Many consumers are seeking the easy solution to their problems in education, psychotherapy, religion, soap-powders, or any of the combinations. And as we daily function as helpers, we meet those who are looking for the pill which will ease their anxiety, depression, or will enhance their self-concept and make them feel better about themselves. We do not have such a pill; nor does anyone else. To live a life of integrity in which one has full measure of joy and sorrow, pain and health is a complex process. Life is not easy and it is not susceptible to the easy-answer pill.

It is our goal to help people who are confronting the complex problems of life. We honor them and life best by not distorting by simplification. Thus, we help people *through* life rather than *around* it.

Today in too many places the simple answer reigns! In religion, people are looking back toward traditional verities; education is running "back to basics"; and in psychology the Human Potential Movement, which would include such groups or movements or techniques as est, Scientology, Rolfing, Primal Therapy, encounter therapies, sex therapies, Bioenergetics, Astrotravel, Arica, Metaphysics, Sentics, Transactional Analysis, Hypnotherapy, Gestalt Therapy, Meditation, pyramid-power, and others, are preaching and teaching "awareness." Some of this is cathartic and useful. However, purification and simplification are different processes and must be separated. Whenever a new religion, educational panacea, psychological technique or advertisement fits the model in this book or suggests that it has the answer for your life, we believe it dishonors both you and the complexity of life.

Our philosophy is simple: We are hooked on life, in all of its grandeur and its depths. We respect and even love the complicated process which is a human life. And our anger is great when anything—be it advertising for automobiles, clothes, new or improved education, religion, or psychotherapy—tries to simplify what is, in fact, complicated and beautiful.

In this book we have focused on the Human Potential Movement, but the model will fit any product which corrupts the beauty of life. As you explore with us what man hath wrought and the assumptions of the new gods, please be ready to shout with us: "P.S. NO MORE B.S.!"

1

Assumptions:

Diarrhea in the Growth Movement

The psychology consumer, like the grocery shopper and the person who seeks to fight the underarm battle, is bombarded with advertising, word of mouth profundity, and the "new, improved giant economy size" packaging process of the Madison Avenue hype. We live on the field of battle. We have difficulty coping with an increasingly complex world and its demands on us. Yet the assistance offered, be it psychology or religion or detergent, may only compound our problems. What to buy is now the question for the consumer. Now that we have the time and money and will, how can we choose between twenty-one different flavors? Would two regular sizes be a better bargain than the giant economy size? Is the stick form of deodorant loger lasting than the aerosol can? Overchoice may be no choice at all.

Consumer education is the new game in town. And now, as the growth of new improved psychologies threatens, the consumer of the mental health package may desire assistance.

What began as a therapeutic movement in psychology has developed into a severe case of diarrhea. Group movements and techniques are spreading faster than the imagination. It is almost as if the imagination is being tested. For example, group therapy grew into weekend-group therapy which grew into nude-weekend-group therapy which will grow into heaven-only-knows-what-comes-next therapy. The body psychologic is racked with pain.

Just as in medicine, where now the cost of the doctor's cure is almost as painful as the disease, the spread of psychologies, purporting to cure or to make you more "aware," is creating more problems for the consumer. The original ideas, to escape the confines of behaviorism and the nightmares of psychoanalysis, were, perhaps, therapeutic; but now to relieve emotional constipation, we have a diarrhea of cure-alls. We have, in a phrase, the psychological trots!

Our goal is *crap detection*. Our goal is to help you help yourself.

Power

Politics pervades our lives. There are the politics of sales and advertising as well as the politics of the Emotional Growth Movement. The question is: Who has the power? The underarm deodorant king's implied message is: Without "Thrush," the new twenty-four-year protection, you will not be safe. Further implication is: If you don't use our product, you won't be the best you can be. If you have to worry about your underarm smell or the ring around your collar, you may also begin to doubt your success quotient or, perhaps, you may have to worry about your womanhood or manhood. Drive on our tires—or worry!

> If you love your family, you will make them brush with Glump!

> If you wish to stay young and slim, you had better drink Slurp!

The message is clear: Without _____ you are less.

And what is good for detergents and cars is good for the con games of emotional growth. The message of too many of the new, improved fads is clear: Without us you are less. To become more aware, take our course. To calm yourself, revitalize yourself, make friends faster, become a leader, understand people better, get in touch with your feelings, foster improved family communication, love your body, massage your mind, "get-it," and (now, here is *The* message) *to be better than you are, you need us.*

The issue is: *Power*. The question is: Who has it? The underarm deodorant salesman and the Emotional Growth Movement guru both want power over you. When the assumption is that I've got something you need, then the game is called one-upmanship. It is the old missionary game. The true believers took "the Word" to the unknowing natives. And when this happened, the price tag read: Power.

This powerful/powerless political perception is not only simplistic, it is also dangerous. When a psychological fad, under the guise of self-improvement, actually is trying to create new adherents, new disciples, or new dependents, then you risk losing the self you wanted to improve.

The hidden issue in all evangelism is power. Although this one-upmanship game is widespread, its dangers are real. When the teacher plays the role of the pitcher of milk, and tries to fill all the little glasses that come into her class, then this is another version of the missionary game. The issue here is, also, power. When the minister attempts to guide the misguided, the issue is power. And when a self-improvement "expert" offers the answer for your life, the issue here in many cases is also Power. If you need or are dependent upon something I have, then like the proverbial button, I have power over you.

It is an old problem with a new twist. "Are you a man or a mouse?" the girl would ask her date as the bully kicked sand in his face in the ad. What choice is there here? What male would say happily, "Mouse"?

Parents stare at the misbehaving child and ask: "When are you going to grow up?" Is this a multiple choice test? True–false? Do I have a choice? Are you still beating your wife?

The issue is Power. The game is one-upmanship. The question is: Who is going to be dependent upon whom? We are suggesting that the new emotional growth, religious, and psycho-religious fads become actually dangerous when two things happen:

1. When they are packaged by the slicks so that they represent themselves as *the answer* for your life.

2. When they offer you a *new dependency* to replace your old ones.

When the salesman—whether he be selling detergents, religion, or psychology—offers a new rendition of "Give me your tired, your poor, your huddled self," beware. He is offering a new dependency. He is asking you not to just give, but to give up control of yourself. The message is: At present, you are inadequate; you need what I am selling.

As you are, you are *not* OK. I have what you need. This is the B.S. message. At this point, your crap detector may be going wild. That is also the politics of personal growth. And inherent in every political transaction is the rip-off factor:

> When the package perpetuates itself at the expense of individual freedom, you are being ripped-off.

> When the consumer substitutes one dependency for another, he or she has just bought a new, one-owner Edsel.

This book offers an alternative to "the answer and new dependency" model. We are offering the politics of self; we are offering individual free choice. We do not believe in *the answer* and we do not feel comfortable with dependent relationships. We are suggesting that:

- You take some pride in the heroics of daily life.

- You try to live through and learn from life itself— in all of its magnitude, charm, love, and pain.

- You have faith in the *cha-cha* formula of living. Most peoples' lives are filled with both mountains and valleys. We progress; we retreat. We take two steps forward; we go back two steps. Cha-cha living is normal, healthy living.

This is not to say that many of us do not need help when we are dwelling in the valley. We do, and we shall need assistance in the future. But helping you to help yourself is different from the packaging of "new and improved" whose primary concern is the perpetuation and profit of the package. The producers of Glump detergent don't promise to clean your clothes today and then go out of business. And neither do most of the human potential, religious, and psycho-religious movements. They are packaged in order to create their own need and to create a continuing need in you. So, the line is drawn. We are suggesting:

> That if any movement, religion, or therapy does not eventually lead you back to yourself, to eventual self-control, then it is strictly B.S. and should be avoided.
>
> That you buy from those who stand ready to self-destruct after helping you become independent of them.
>
> That you avoid those movements whose bottom line is not you.

Expectations

The consciousness revolution exists and grows in a society which is charged with developing expectations. We expect many things under the rubric of the "good life" and we are impatient with fulfillment. Time has become our most precious commodity.

We expect all services to be delivered quickly. If the doctor is slow in diagnosing our illnesses, we change doctors. If we must go into the hospital, our first question generally is: How long will we be there? And, if we find ourselves with a psychologist, we expect solution or absolution quickly. We go to our TV repairman, our church, doctor, psychologist or new guru with the same expectations: the quick answer.

Too many times the power of the con-game gurus is used to perpetuate their own existence, rather than to free you. Too many times the growth industry offers band-aids to people with deep emotional lacerations. And too many times the techniques and elements of concentration camp brainwashing are used under the rubric of personal growth.

The Emotional Growth Movement may be the Band-Aid Man of emotional life. Do you have a cut? Put a Band-Aid on it. Is your appendix hurting? Put a Band-Aid on it. Are you suffering from ulcers? A Band-Aid will fix you up.

Americans believe in band-aids and consume them in great numbers. Instant cure. Instant happiness. And since many parts of the Emotional Growth Movement are assuming the band-aid posture, they, too, are being consumed in large numbers.

The con-games of emotional growth have joined the instant-cure bandwagon. One current fad offers its course in only two weekends. A small price in time to "get it" is the implication. There are marathon groups, weekend groups, one-day courses, one week courses, three-hours-with-the-guru affairs. Part of this instant philosophy is a corollary to the consumer-is-always-right dictum, and, since the consumer now wants instant coffee, cocoa and pleasure, she also wants instant emotional growth. However, when the

Emotional Growth Movement offers its wares in instant packaging it risks simplification and, therefore, irrelevancy. Instant everything has solved few of our problems—from thirst to growth. When you, the consumer, want the answer, and want it now, you run the risk of only getting *now's* answer.

We, as a society, have developed high expectations for ourselves as people. Sin, to speak generically, is no longer certain evil; sin is the doubt or guilt resulting from not living up to our own expectations. Men expect to be "good" fathers and communicate constantly and sufficiently with their children; women are supposed to be nurturing mothers; our children are expected to cause a minimum of inconvenience and to give us a maximum amount of pride and joy. When we are defeated by our own expectations, we have become our own enemy. Perhaps our sense of perfection is both a cross and an incentive, but too many times we miss the pain of cross-bearing, and assume individual guilt. And the resulting paradox reinforces the message of the B.S. movements, which is: You are not OK as you are. The individual accepts this judgment, then creates further expectations, which, in turn, are self-defeating. The bottom line of this circular maelstrom of impatience and self-defeating expectations is that we become fair game for the B.S. package which is merchandising monsters who use our vulnerability against us, and which perpetuates our dependent postures.

Now that we have delineated the politics of personal growth and drawn a picture of the victims of this power struggle, let us go one more step and define the battle lines even more clearly. Let us examine some of the basic philosophical assumptions, some or all of which form the basis of such diverse movements as evangelical religion, body/mind therapies, analytical models and interpersonal growth groups. It is this book's contention that some of these assumptions are misleading and, perhaps, harmful, and may lead to the rip-off factor in that the individual is relegated to victim—a powerless posture rather than final arbiter of his or her own life. Finally, we shall offer our own set of alternative philosophical assumptions, which may shed new light on unchallenged premises.

Assumptions

Many of the emotional growth fads and those movements which combine characteristics of both psychology and religion, share at least some of the following assumptions and promises. Their collective message is:

> If you will take our course, join our
>   group, or become a convert, you will
> Develop hidden unused potential
> Gain a sense of purpose and direction
> Grow as a person
> Gain greater awareness of self and
> become more "self-actualized"
> Find a place where you can be yourself,
>   where you are accepted as you are
> Learn effective communication skills
> Be able to avoid future conflict
> Gain a new sense of the meaning of life

It is our contention that the foregoing assumptions, when left unexamined, form the boundaries of B.S. They are promises which are often unrealistic, and they may easily lead us into spiraling expectations again. We shall question these assumptions and suggest that the realities are often very different than the promises. All we need to do is to take a closer look.

You will develop hidden unused potential

It is your basic true–false test. Question: Does every person have hidden, unused potential? Your answer is: True _____ False _____

If you answered True, then you may be vulnerable to the con. You may have already bought the assumptions of B.S. The point is that hidden, unused potential is an assumption, not necessarily a fact. It is home remedy raised to the level of medicinal legitimacy. We have seldom stopped to ask, does everyone have hidden potential? Do some people use one hundred percent of their potential, and, therefore, have no reservoir for improvement? What if you don't have hidden potential; does that mean you are not OK?

This hidden, unused potential assumption can lead directly to a state of dissatisfaction. What better way to make a person feel uneasy about himself than to tell him he is not living up to his potential? Assuming an unused potential within everyone is an excellent way to create an audience of dissatisfied people, "They" will develop your potential. Watch out! In too many cases their essential message is: Be different than you are. The issue is the politics of change. *Who is going to control your life? Who is going to define "potential" for you? Who is going to dic-tate the goal of change?* Beware the gift-bearing guru who promises to help you "develop your po-tential." His assumptions, hidden behind that phrase, may dirty your feet.

You will gain a sense of purpose and direction

This may be true. Many of the "pop" move-ments offer a blue print for your life and expect you to follow blindly. Through this you may well gain a sense of purpose and direction. The ques-tion is: Whose purpose and direction? The result is too often severe dependency which does not result in a freeing sense, but in a crippling stance.

You will grow as a person

"Growth" is the most important word in the lexicon of human potential. There are "growth centers" whose reason for existence is the pro-motion of growth through expanded awareness. There are personal growth courses, methods, techniques and training. The goal is growth. And with this goal we have no argument. However, too often there is single mindedness and over-simplification which brings to mind the famous scene in the movie "The Graduate," when Dustin Hoffman is told the secret of life by a well-mean-ing businessman: "Plastics." It is as if an entire psychological and social movement is built around a ghost. The secret word is "growth." Growth is a warm fuzzy. Who can be against it? Can you imagine Mrs. Smith saying, "No, I don't want to grow; I wish to stagnate."? Perhaps we can! Has anyone considered that stagnation might be constructive? Personal growth is an *assumed* good. Institutional growth generally assumes money. Beware the warm fuzzies; what you see may not be what you get.

You will gain a greater awareness of self and become more "self-actualized"

Is "awareness of self" really what you want? No one has really stopped to ask: Is awareness always a desirable end? We suggest: Not necessarily. True, awareness can bring much fulfillment and joy but also much pain and grief. Some components of the Emotional Growth Movement would have you believe that awareness is always synonymous with growth. Bullshit! Growth is growth, and awareness is awareness, and perhaps never the twain shall meet. Let's not be dazzled by this footwork; words are not necessarily realities.

If we were traveling, we might have to stop and ask directions to Self-Actualization City. Where is it? What is it? Will we know it when we get there? Once upon a time a psychologist suggested that a healthy person should be striving for self-actualization. A movement built up around this idea. Now, actualization is one of the great shoulds of emotional growth, and it may also be one of the great road blocks to the acceptance of self. The band-aid has become the problem.

You will find a place where you can be yourself, where you are accepted as you are

You are not accepted as you are in many of

these groups. Each group has many unspecified, but real norms. You will be judged by your participation, intensity of belief or support of the group's life. Therefore, these groups become little different from society itself. People do not change magically or suspend being human just because they are in an interpersonal awareness class or pseudo-psycho-religious training program. You will most likely be judged, and judgments are a far distance from acceptance.

You will learn effective communication skills

They will help you communicate better. B.S.! Your new-found lingo may, in fact, hinder communication outside the group. The result in too many cases is an in-group feeling, a division of the world into *innies* and *outies*, which results in a personal isolation. You may, in fact, be worse off than before. You may have a new way of talking, with no one to talk to.

You will be able to avoid future conflicts

If you take this course, begin meditating, or believe deeply enough, you will be able to avoid future conflict. Oh, the assumptions run wild! Is conflict always bad? Can't conflict sometimes bring people together? Might not hate be tinged with love? It is arrogantly assumed by some parts of the Emotional Growth Movement that conflict between people is bad. It is *ass*-umed; and that *ass*-umption is asinine. An absence of conflict is not necessarily the goal of life. Perhaps we need some conflict in our lives, if we are to grow, change, become reflective, and develop.

We suggest that Camelot is not a land in which to live; when the Camelot realtor calls, beware his assumptions.

You will gain a new sense of the meaning of life

Many parts of the Emotional Growth Movement and psycho-religious groups claim to make sense of life for you. There is danger here. Essentially this is an external offering which does not always leave one with the internal mechanism for making sense of the world. As we said, if the bottom line is not you, it is a rip-off. You, the consumer, should beware of others' desires to "make sense" for you; we believe you can do it yourself.

An encyclopedia salesman lives on every block; there are used car salesmen on every corner. And there are those—whether they call themselves teachers, gurus, therapists, leaders, ministers, or counselors—who wish to sell Camelot pills. The easy answer is for sale. Deception is available. *Assumptions pose as facts.* There is a constant rip-off possibility in a psychological Camelot.

There is diarrhea in many areas of the consciousness revolution today. New fads are born, instant gurus are made, self-help courses and books proliferate; everybody seems to have the answer for your life. This book, however, does not claim to be a panacea or an answer book. To paraphrase an old joke: With this book and a quarter, you can buy a cup of coffee. That is a possibility. Or, with this book you can save yourself hundreds of dollars and hours of anguish. The authors simply believe you may desire some assistance as you walk through the psychological marketplace. Your personal crap detector may need sharpening. This book, therefore, can be used as a first step into the marketplace. We do not say: Don't buy the new, emotional growth psychologies. We say: Know and question what you are buying.

2

Needs:

Noisy Desperation

The plays of our lives:

> *Scene I*: The advertisement reads: "Florida Real
> Estate. Cheap." The advertisement ran in maga-
> zines, newspapers and is painted on billboards for
> all to see. It does not tell the whole story, which
> includes the fact that the real estate lies beneath a
> swamp and is the present home of alligators.

Comment: This scene was too true a few years
ago. The dreams of the every day folk were
abused and taken advantage of.

> *Scene II*: On almost any corner in America sits
> Harry's Used Cars. And Harry or Roy or Ed are
> out to sell you a "Nice. Clean. One-owner. . . ."
> Or, the car he has for you was owned by a little old
> lady, who only drove it on Sundays, and whose be-
> loved son was a mechanic. The scenario is written
> every day, on almost every corner. Need has been
> created and there are those ready to make money
> on your needs.

Comment: This is the classic American rip-off.

> *Scene III*: Mr. and Mrs. and Ms. American sit
> before their television set. The work day is over.
> Supper dishes are done. They should be at their
> ease. Yet they are uneasy. The women move about
> the house, constantly "doing." The man remains
> in front of the television, while his mind mean-
> ders between a cabin on the lake, moving to Cali-
> fornia, his dreams for the kids, where he is now
> and how he got that way. His body becomes rest-
> less. At the commercial break all three line up at
> the bathroom.

Comment: Past dreams and present realities do
not mesh.

For many of us, our lives are not equal to our
dreams. In school, Sara saw herself as a nurse;
she is a housewife. John was going to own his
own business; he is paid by the hour. Where did
those dreams, visions of bright futures, go? What
happened to those people who were able to
dream?

Ask Sam, the used car king, if he, as a young
man, dreamed of selling used cars on the corner.
Sam will probably answer "No." His dreams
were of making money, deals, excitement. When
pressed, he may admit to a secret wish to drive in
the Indianapolis 500 or at Le Mans or Monte
Carlo. But then Sam will shrug away what he has
come to believe are idealistic or "pipe" dreams.
He has learned to be content with Sam's Used
Cars and the smaller goals of economic
security—sending the kids to college, a good
home, and, hopefully, a decent marriage.

Even the real estate bird who was trying to
sell you the ten acres of honest-to-god swamp

land would, in a quieter time, admit to dreams in banking or perhaps he saw himself as chief executive of an important corporation. No, our Florida real estate tycoon never dreamed of being what he is—a rip-off artist.

We are our dreams, yet somehow our lives have not measured up to our dreams. Many of us live compromise lives, and many more seem to be living lives with no certain direction. Is there an explanation for how a young man who wants to drive at Indy ends up selling used cars? How does nice little Johnny Smith become John Smith, Swamp Salesman? Whatever happened to our dreams?

These questions have begun to dominate our idle moments. And our realities are being dominated by the noisy answers put forward by the society which helped manufacture the dreams and the questions. Depending on where you live, you are doubtless offered "lake property" or "vacationland" in the Green Mountains, the Appalachian Mountains, the Ozarks, Rockies, Florida, or California. With a small sum down and monthly payments you too can match your dreams with reality. So you buy the property of your dreams. Now the television set or billboards or newspapers or magazines bombard your anxious reality with the apparently obvious fact that you don't smell right, use the correct deodorant, drive the right car, have the best chick/dude, or clean your house with the right sweeper or furniture polish. *Drive me! Drink me! Wash with me! Smell with me!*

Answers multiply. Gestation period is overnight.

We are a people whose dreams and realities do not match. Perhaps we are victims of rising expectations in dreamland. Still, the resulting frustration, anxiety, sense of unfulfillment is real and painful. And the quickest diagnosis has come from the hucksters of products in America. Our needs, real and created, stand ready to be met. And, having taken that last logical, if not moral, step, Barnumesque America stands ready to create the needs it can fulfill.

Florida Real Estate!
Cheap Land in Nevada!
Nice . . . one owner . . . used cars.

P. T. Barnum, meet Mr. and Mrs. and Ms. Average American!

So, are we surprised when those restless people with anxieties and suffering from vague dis-ease turn to psychology for solutions? We should not be. Given a culture based on insecurity, it is logical to predict the growth of psychologies. Nor should we be surprised when the part-time Edsel dealer offers "psychological" possibilities. That is the model: *psychology sells!*

"Come one, come all," cry the purveyors of psychological panaceas. "We promise to answer all your questions! We promise to lead you into the promised land of Health, Happiness, and Success!"

This point must not be missed: What is implied in the selling of deodorants, automobiles or land is also implied in the selling of psychology. And what exactly is implied? *Sim-*

plification. Solution. Answers. The way to bring dreams and realities closer together.

The noise of the proliferating answers can drown out your questions.

> *Buy me* and your identity problems will be solved.
> *Be a student* of this technique.
> *Come* to a conference on _____
> *Take lessons in* _____
> *Learn* _____

Answers multiply. Answers are manufactured. Answers resound.

Questions remain.

Personal anxiety, insecurity, and restlesness are complex phenomena, twin rooted, perhaps, in the human unconscious and the impact of culture. To simplify this complexity by offering "drive-in psychology," "instant cure," or "quick answers" is demeaning to both psychology and to the psychology consumer.

The questions: Who am I? Where am I going? How? Why? Can this "I" cope? are serious and ongoing. These are the stuff of dreams. And their answerable realities must evolve from a synthesis of opportunity, personal skills, sweat, vision, persistence, and a myriad of other factors which together make up a human life. To the extent that psychology reveres this synthesis process and strives to enhance it, psychology honors its consumers and succeeds. To the extent that growth psychology simplifies the human play, it fails and dishonors itself and those it claims to serve.

The Florida real estate salesman, Used Car

Ed, and psychology share both the noise of the answer and the desperation of the questions.

None of this is to suggest, however, that real people do not have real concerns or confront real issues. They do. We do. Sometimes we are bored, lonely, empty; we feel set apart or alienated from those and that around us; our families break under the strain and leave us floating in confusion; we search for a sense of roots; and to be able to get up each morning and cope with what our days bring, we live examined lives. We ask, each in our own way: Who am I? What do I want out of life? How can I be happier? How can I risk loving? Where am I going – and finally – What is life all about?

All of this is what living is about. To breathe is to sometimes ponder the irrationality of our individual "fates," and their capriciousness. And no matter who you are, simple brave or Indian chief, your garden will have a certain number of thorns in it. Wish that it were not true, but it is so.

However, we are suggesting that there is a vast difference between *real* needs and those that are contrived by you or by those to whom you look for answers. A feeling of *noisy desperation* pervades the land. I am alone! We are bored, afraid! What is happening to us? My life is meaningless! What is the answer?

As we whisper, our collective noise is all-consuming. We do not need to contrive or create problems for ourselves. Yet, still we do. As we desperately whisper, we constantly seek not only new answers but new questions as well. It is as if we enjoy desperation.

Thus, paradoxically, there seems to be a simultaneous search for new answers and a disbelief in new answers. We are holding on to our questions, while the noise of answers increases. Perhaps there is more comfort and less risk in questions than in answers.

Perversely perhaps, we remain fertile ground for the "answer planter." New products have a ready market in us. New detergent—new way to wash. New religion—new true believers. New psychology—new disciples. And disciples we are because we hunger for the new, giant economy size savior to lead us into the Promised Land. We look for this "teacher" in detergents, automobiles, and growth movements. That is the new religion: in general, *belief has become not the means to an end, but the end itself*. We are believers. We search for answers. We seek. We are on the move.

The precariousness of a faith which focuses on means and not ends is obvious. It, and its believers, are vulnerable to all winds from every direction. And, ultimately, we become our own worst enemy, for we build castles of expectations in the skies of the mind, and when we cannot live there we build new ones, higher and more elaborate. We are a believing people.

For many of us, traditional religion no longer adequately deals with our questions and our searching. We have sought answers in strange packages. Thousands, if not millions, are turning to that part of psychology which promises *the answer* and promises to lead us to the Promised Land. To the extent that we believe in promised lands, we are fools. And to the extent we contrive needs which new "teachers" can fulfill, we participate in our own degradation.

> The emotional growth salesman is culpable when he promises us a land beyond the river.
>
> We are our own enemies when we seek to be led across the river.
>
> Yes, part of the noise you hear is real. Real people have real needs and are calling for real help. But out there, also, are salesmen who are trying to create a market for left-handed, psychological monkey wrenches. And we are out there—noisy in our desperation—often seeking synthetic solutions to natural problems.

Power becomes the central issue. We often take the easy way and manipulate others. Psychology responds to our needs by assuming authority for our lives. We and psychology both lose when the issue of power is either overlooked or understated.

Tear Power —
or
How to Manipulate Through Weakness

Weakness is power. That is the subliminal message of our culture, growth psychology, and many "awareness" consumers. Do not be deceived. Their words, and our's, say just the opposite. We are supposedly a power seeking people. We live in a culture based on power. Emotional growth psychology preaches the power of the person. Watch out: there is built-in irony here. The world is turned upside down. Lilliputians rule the world! Weakness is power!

Very early in life, a female learns the power of tears. When all else fails, cry. She learns that tears gain her power in the family, and especially she learns that Daddy and Brother hate to see girls cry.

If tears don't work, she switches to the oh-you-big-handsome-brute tactic. She plays helpless and when he does it for her, she gushes breathlessly, "Oh, you big handsome brute," or a synonymous expression. He feels ten feet tall and she has the power.

So little Suzy learns to control the men in her life. She manipulates them through tear power. Control the gland, control the man!

Yes the preceding is a stereotype of women, and yes, it is a cliche. But both stereotypes and cliches become so because of the accuracy inherent in them. Also, women have not had a lock on the concept of weakness as power. Early in their careers as males, boys learn to manipulate through weakness. "I can't" became the expression of helplessness. "I can't" was power. Mother did it for you. That was and is child power. Wife does it for you now—husband power.

The Emotional Growth Movement offers goodies to the helpless and many consumers are grabbing. Although it proclaims the opposite, the emphasis on "growth," in fact, rewards tears and teaches us that power is achieved through helplessness. Its subtle message is, too often: Desperation is Good!

The litany of growth psychology says: "Be open. Admit your problems. See that you are a victim." This openness to weakness is called health. Assurance is the goody. If you are "open" to your weakness and will talk about it, you are assured you are mentally healthy. You are OK. Recognition is power.

Another goody is a sense of belonging. If you are weak, you are one of "us." To be fulfilled or content is to be alone. To be searching or "trying" is to be like the rest of us. And, since you are one of us, we want to help you. Mind expansion groups become support groups. Patients become students or clients. And the individual learns that the key to the manipulation of others, the way to be helped, is weakness. The meek *do* inherit, if not the earth. power.

Group facilitator: Now, Sam, would you like to share anything with the group?

Sam: No.

First Member: Well, what makes you so special? The rest of us have been open.

Sam: I am being open with you, I have nothing to say.

Second Member: Aw, come on, Sam, just tell us about your problems.

Sam: I don't have any problems?

First Member: No problems?

Sam: Nothing special. Just the usual.

Second Member: Well, if you don't have any problems, why are you here?

Sam: I was just curious.

Third Member: Curious? That's not good enough. Curious just doesn't make it. Curious. . .

First Member: Yeah, that's right. You got to be more than curious. You got to have problems . . . like the rest of us.

Sam: Sorry. I was just curious.

Facilitator: I'm afraid we'll have to ask you to leave, Sam. Your presence is not helping the group.

As Sam leaves, a voice says: "Gee, is that guy screwed up!" "Yeah," another answers, "He sure has got lots of problems." "Right," a third says, "He has a long way to go before he will be open enough to join a group like this."

A third goody is reward. Many groups within the Emotional Growth Movement expect the initiate to recognize that without their message, course, or techniques his life is screwed up. As soon as he "sees the light," he is admitted into the flock. He is rewarded.

Do not miss the religious symbolism here; for that is exactly what it is. Religion, in the generic sense, preaches turning the other cheek, the concept of sinner, the meek being rewarded, humility as posture. All of these, it is said, are the ways to power. Emotional growth psychology, on the other hand, espouses openness, expression of "real" feelings, the concept of weakness, and mental health as a reward for recognizing your messed-up state. Yes, religion and growth psychology are philosophical neighbors. Their rituals differ, yet the pay-offs are similar. Ultimately, in both, the search is the pay-off and the pay-off is in the search. Amen.

There is danger in such a psychology. The implication of the message is: Since I am weak and in control, why should I bother to change and grow? Thus, to be strong is to be controlled, to be weak is to control. While I am busy controlling you, I don't have to worry about controlling me. Therefore, this ultimate goal of personal growth, which is to be generally admired, may be defeated by its own message. There are too many goodies for the weak in some growth messages. And there are too many consumers willing to participate in the game.

"I am weak."

"No, that means you are strong."

"You mean, if I'm weak that means I'm strong?"

"Right. You got it."

"But what if I'm strong? Does that mean I'm weak?"

"Hum . . . maybe it does . . ."

"Well, I guess I'll stay weak then, thank you."

Amen.

We suggest: Yes there are *real* needs and *real* answers. Yes, there are *real* needs and *synthetic* answers. And tragically, yes, there are *synthetic* needs and *synthetic* answers.

3

Problems and Solutions:
Cures for What Ails Ya

There are problems

Allen, a successful forty-two-year-old business-man, had become increasingly depressed. He felt his life was meaningless. His wife, job, and children no longer continued to give him satisfaction. Allen's wife attempted to console him by giving sympathy, loving care, and a listening ear. This, he reported, did little good. He continued to feel confused, hopeless and helpless.

Stopping in a bookstore, Allen came across the "self-improvement" section, and discovered over two dozen books suggesting that they contained the answers to the great questions of life. He bought several. Allen's journey began.

Engrossed in his reading, Allen began to make fewer decisions, both at home and on the job. His wife, Judy, accepted the responsibility for handling financial matters, making decisions about the children, making excuses to relatives and friends that Allen didn't want to see, and even accepted his suggestion that all he needed was an extramarital affair to help "clear his mind." Ah, the benefits of confusion!

In the meantime, Allen enrolled in a workshop entitled "Knowing Yourself Through Emotional Energy," and discovered many other people who also felt confused about their lives and were ready to be "enlightened." Only one problem: Three weeks after the group ended the enlightenment wore off and confusion set in again.

Next came "Scream Therapy" (scream your confusion away for $150 a day). Allen never felt so alive—that is, for about six weeks.

Back at home, Judy strongly suspected Allen was having an affair with one of his fellow enlightenment seekers. However, she understood— he's confused and "going through a lot." She had become used to making excuses for him. His friends understood and made a point of calling to console Allen every chance they got. After all, he's confused. Allen had become familiar with many offerings within the Emotional Growth Movement. He exposed himself further to interpersonal awareness groups. "Astro-travel," marathons, sexual experimentation workshops and "body alignment" sessions. Allen is now happy but still confused. Why is he happy? Allen has learned there is strength in confusion, power in weakness, and control in helplessness.

Addie is twenty. She has had five jobs in two years. She doesn't want to go to college, but she hasn't liked any of her jobs either. She has thought of traveling, but is still here. She has considered marriage, but thinks she is too young. Addie has been sampling bits of life, but she has no direction for her life.

That is, until she discovered the Church of Science. After attending an introductory lecture, Addie decided she would enroll in two or three sessions to get "clear." After eighteen months, Addie is still a member of the Church of Science, has spent her life savings of four thousand dollars for "clearing sessions" and is now about to try to secure a loan for two thousand dollars more. Addie now has direction for her life. And the Church of Science has a new lifetime member.

Jim and Linda were happily married, or so they thought. Several months ago a friend of Linda's suggested she enroll in a two weekend course of self-awareness and self-improvement. After some discussion, Linda decided to send in her $300 and to "see what's it all about." To her surprise, there were two hundred and fifty other people attending the same program that weekend. Packed into a large ballroom, participants were instructed to take a seat in one of the perfectly lined. hard-backed chairs.

During the course of the sixty-hour training program, several interesting things happened to Linda. She was called a "turkey" and "asshole" by the leader, not allowed to use the restroom when she asked permission, subjected to having the participant next to her throw up (he was made to clean the mess up himself), "stared down" by the leader in front of the other 249 members, and bored to tears by hours of long lectures on the workings of the mind. However, by the end of the workshop she had "gotten it." It was just as the leader had told her, they all had been "ripped off" because what they had learned was what they had known all along: "What is, is and what ain't, ain't."

Linda, now feeling as though she was fully responsible for her life, went back home to Jim where she shared her new experiences and promptly informed him that she was filing for divorce. Stunned, Jim clearly didn't "get it."

There Are Solutions

The supermarket of solutions to life's questions under the rubric of "emotional growth" offers a wide variety of techniques, exercises and philosophies, few of which are offered at discount costs. Most of these, however, can be grouped into the following categories:

>Eastern philosophies
>Quasi-religions
>Interpersonal awareness groups
>Body-mind therapies
>Analytical models

Let us perfunctorily examine these categories of the Emotional Growth Movement, which purport to solve our problems or to show us the way to enlightenment and fulfillment.

Eastern Philosophies

The *Eastern philosophies* generally do not call themselves therapies, but ways of life. They emphasize profound utterings of gurus, prophets, of teachers, and they offer spiritual en-

lightenment about the laws of the universe. Meditation and breathing are key processes, often
combined with sitting in difficult physical postures while contemplating the merging of self.
The primary goal usually involves expanding
awareness internally and externally while trans-
cending the intellect in order to understand all.

Quasi-religions

Psychology and religion have created off-
shoot children which borrow from both parents
but are neither totally. We call these groups
quasi-religion. Their goals are to expand consciousness or "get clear." Getting control of your
mind is also a goal. Some of these groups, which
do consider themselves therapeutic, offer "psy-
chocalisthenics" to get the body to think; visualization techniques which will improve your life
control; mind projections, and courses which
will "center" you by peeling off layers of your
psychic onion. These groups offer both self-
knowledge and religious salvation to their
believers or students.

Interpersonal awareness groups

Another thread in the emotional growth
fabric is that of *interpersonal awareness*. These
groups, varying in time from one hour a week to
weekend marathons (with or without clothes) try
to foster communication between people. A participant may come to see how he is seen by
others. General guidelines include speaking only
for yourself, staying in the "here and now," making statements instead of asking questions, willingness to self-disclose, and giving and receiv-

ing feedback. Often, extreme emotional exchanges occur during the course of a group's life. Also the group can offer support to the individual who wishes to change.

Body-mind therapies

A fourth thread is what we call the *body-mind therapies*. These courses or techniques have in common a belief in the direct relationship between the body and the mind. Most manipulate the body in some way, from slow, simple exercises which claim to work with gravitational stress to the deep and painful massaging of hands, feet, backs and faces. These body therapies suggest that emotions are stored within the body, and if these deposits can be loosened through exercise or manipulation then the person can become more aware emotionally and more in control.

Another component of body-mind therapies is the assumption that feelings about past events are also stored up and need to be dissolved or dealt with. Techniques are offered which try to break down one's present body "armor" and to return one to an emotional past. A participant might be asked to confront, scream at, or tell off a person from his past. Or, participants might be found crying on the floor like babies, hitting walls, or beating pillows. These techniques often see the body as energy potential, and they attempt to release stored energy or to balance body energy. Participants are trained in visualization techniques, physical exercises, or martial arts systems. All techniques are designed for catharsis and expanded awareness.

Analytical Models

The final thread of the human potential fabric is what we call the *analytical models*. These courses generally offer new ways to look at the world. They sometimes use a new language, which might include such phrases as "energy flow," "get it," "ego states," or "clearing." And they may or may not require marathon weekends in order to expand one's awareness.

The Emotional Growth Movement, including quasi-religions, is a broad cloth which covers many forms, components, and techniques. Both number and form increase daily. And it is to these solutions that many of us turn with our problems. As you read this, are you saying to yourself, "Hey, I'm one of these people," or, "I know someone this is happening to." If so, you may already know the enemy. We are our own enemies and sometimes our solutions become part of the problem, not part of the answer.

If a stranger were to visit your town or city, he or she might read about burglaries and other crimes, but as he drove the streets he would not be able to see the pain that lies behind the closed doors of the houses. Perhaps we are victims of our own rising expectations, and therefore, our own enemy. Or perhaps the realities of life in our cities cause not comfort but pain. Whatever the reason, the fact is that there is much personal suffering going on out there in television land.

Life is a rip-off for some folks.

Too many are bleeding behind closed doors.

Too many are being hurt by those to whom they look for help.

There is pain here.

Please Convince Me I'm OK

One of the most prolific myths in American history is that of the outsider who comes to save the townfolk. Matt Dillon comes to clean up Dodge City. The salesman travels through with his remedies for what ails us. The itinerant preacher comes to marry us and bury us. The outsider, being not one of us, is distrusted yet yearned for.

The Emotional Growth Movement today is filled with "garbage" words—those words which are vague in meaning or have so many definitions they become meaningless. The most used yet abstruse of these is "growth." We are confronted with "personal growth," "emotional growth," "academic growth," and ad infinitum growth! We are suffering beneath an adjectival explosion and a concomitant growth profusion. Stocks grow! Plants grow! People grow! This is surely the "growing" season.

Another factor in this game of growth is that we have yet to define the differences between "change" and "growth." Admittedly personal growth in emotional terms is one of those gray areas which decry preciseness. Also, growth is a value-laden term which, therefore, is susceptible to individual manipulation. Growth to one person is simply change to another. For example, if one shows more emotion and, as a result, is more openly angry toward family and friends, is this growth? Or, suppose a wife has a growth experience in a therapy group, then returns home to divorce her husband; is this growth? Personal growth is a warm-fuzzy. Personal growth is like Beethoven's music—it sounds good, but we often don't understand it.

The result is: Change has become synonymous with growth. If you are different, you have grown; if I can see a change in you, you have grown. As a society, we confuse change with progress; as individuals we define growth as change.

Now, if we put these two threads together—seeking the outsider who has the answer for our problems and the philosophical illusion of growth—we have a concept which might be called the Lone Ranger syndrome. A masked man rides into town, sizes up the situation, solves any problem we have, then rides off into the sunset. It is a common theme; the Lone Ranger syndrome is part of our history and belief structure.

The implication inherent in a belief in psychological Lone Rangers is that the townfolk are inadequate. Or, that the townfolk see themselves as helpless and inadequate. If George, the hardware store owner, could run off the badmen, he wouldn't need the Lone Ranger. If the bank could protect itself, it wouldn't need the outsider. If we could handle our own problems, we would not need that masked man and his sidekick Indian. So, as grateful as the townfolk are, they are also resentful and angry. They have seen their own limitations and, although saved, would eventually turn against their saviours. The Lone Ranger and Tonto are mirrors for the town, and mirrors in which the folks see a picture of themselves which is not pleasing. The Lone Ranger and Tonto are smart to leave town quickly.

Tonto and "Kimo Sabbe" do not have to live with a sense of failure and, therefore, a yearning for an outsider. They *are* the outsiders and their role in the script is the easier. They ride into town, do good, then ride out. Easy as one, two, three. Tomorrow, a new town. Same script. Theirs is a repetitious life, but easy. The more difficult role is played by the townfolk. First, it is harder to be the debtor. Secondly, after the masked man and the Indian ride out of town, the folks must face tomorrow with a sense of their own inadequacy and a belief in an "outside" solution for their problems.

We have pursued this myth because it is our contention that the differing parts of the Emotional Growth Movement have, in many cases, simultaneously represented themselves as the Lone Ranger and taken advantage of our vulnerability to that figure. They have represented themselves as the answer man asking only: What is the question you wish me to answer.

We townfolk have been vulnerable to the message of the outsider that we are not OK, that we need him, his remedy. The traveling salesman came to Boonville to sell Uncle Bob's Home Remedy and Shoeshine Kit, while disparaging the "local yokels." And he was right! We *were* yokels because we believed in fences and the green grass on the other side. We were yokels because we were victims of our own myths. In order to run Uncle Bob out of town on a rail, we would have to destroy part of ourselves, our cultural fabric. And we did not and do not have the courage to do this. So the townfolk bought Uncle Bob's Home Remedy and Shoeshine Kit, while distrusting the salesman and joking that he better never come near our daughters, lest he wants a seatful of buckshot. And the salesman left town a richer, if not wiser, man.

There is something in us which makes us intolerant of the preciseness of the human condition. To be human is to be precisely filled with pain, suffering, ambivalence, and wrenching questions. To be human is sometimes to be precisely confused. And to be human, as we are, is to believe that someone out there doesn't suffer a fate similar to our own. To be our kind of human is to believe that someone out there has the answers to our questions—hence our vulnerability to the Lone Ranger and to the con games of emotional growth.

Please convince me I'm OK. That is our message to each other. We wish to be different, but not too different. we wish to be alike, but not too much alike. We wish to be affirmed.

Parents are attending parent education courses in great numbers. Their motivation is diverse, but one of the parts is a desire to be affirmed as parents. Although their presence in a class suggests a sense of inadequacy, they want their parenting past to be confirmed.

Many people populate the psychiatrist's couch or the psychologist's office seeking affirmation. We believe in the green grass on the other side of the fence, yet we wish some water and sun for our own scrubby shrubs. We believe and simultaneously disbelieve in the magic of gardeners.

That is part of our ambivalence, and that is our message to each other and to our environment. Through this open door walk the various techniques and philosophies collectively called the Emotional Growth Movement, whose intent is to accentuate our insecurities and to serve them.

The message of what we are calling the con games of emotional growth is: You are not now OK, but after you take our course, participate in this group, etcetera, you will be OK. Present–not OK; future–OK. It is the same "before and after" message of the muscle-building course too many of us males enrolled in as teenagers. We didn't want any bullies kicking sand in our faces! And the message is similar to that of the pimple cream which promised to anxious teens an overnight transformation. This desire and expectation for acceptance and affirmation we exhibited at sixteen is still a part of us. We are still vulnerable. Only the products which fulfill that need change.

4

Leaders
and Methods:
Gurus, Games, and
Gimmicks

Gurus

In every darkness there is a flashlight salesman.
In winter we are sold bathing suits; in summer
we put warm coats in lay-away. Questions not
only provide answers, they provide people with
the answer. If the growth of "growth" psychologies is one of the phenomena of contemporary
culture, then the concomitant growth in the
number of gurus is phenomenal.

For every mudhole there is a Mr. Clean. For
every city there is a Natural Man. For each
patient there is a doctor. For every darkness
there is a great light.

Movements need leaders, by definition. "Hey,
Joe, let's start a movement." "All right. Now who is
going to be the leader?" Every psychology needs a
psychologist. Every religion needs its prophets
and ministers. So, by definition, the proliferating
con-games of emotional growth have created the
need for con-artists. B.S. needs B.S.-ers.

The story is newspaper common. In block letters we read: "Guru calls for mass prayer." There are gurus of sexual awareness, dreams or fantasies; there are encounter gurus; group gurus; there are gurus who have it, are fading it, losing it, brushing their teeth with it. The condition is simple: A guru for every movement, a movement for each guru. And if this condition of the body psychologic can be seen as dis-ease, then we are in for an epidemic.

Psychology is not the only field which suffers the growth of gurus. Religion, for another, has traditionally sought prophets— synthetic, as well as real. Today western religion has accepted the indictment of eastern thought, and, therefore, looks to the rising sun for new gurus. The teenager from India is now exalted into "leader," the sitar-playing itinerant is assumed profound, and anyone who can get into the "lotus" position, let alone stay in it, is assumed to sit at the right hand of God. As the collective American Church wanders through its forty-day wilderness, it looks not only eastward, but inward. The result is the rise of gurus from among us—the boy next door who can now heal by the laying on of hands; the child preacher who talks of sin and, therefore, must know it and, since children do not know sin, must be God inspired; the preacher who reaches millions "out there in radio-land;" the teenager who drives Cadillacs and is the leader of the new Apostolic Razzle Dazzle Church; the New Sun and Old Moon religion captures millions of faithful; the peripatetic preacher who exhorts us to "find Jesus;" the young people who confront us at shopping centers and beseech us to "see the light" or "come and do likewise." Radio-land is filled with people who have the answer. They await those of us who have the questions. Our cup runneth over.

So, the flashlight salesman has found the dark territory. To paraphrase P. T. Barnum again, not only is there a sucker born every minute, but the flashlight salesman knows that there is a child of darkness born each minute, and the salesman has come to enable us to see the light. Hallelujah! Amen! And pass the salt.

The authors of this book are not necessarily against all flashlight salesmen. The growth of gurus comes with the dark territory. We may be stuck with gurus through the definition of movements. What we are promoting, however, is a perception and recognition of the underlying issue of power. Beneath each movement and every guru is the question: Who has the power? The existence of gurus assumes a powerful and powerless dichotomy—students and teachers, leaders and those who are led. Gurus create followers. Gurus need followers. And to follow, one must give up power. To be a true follower, one must give up autonomy and control over oneself.

The issue behind the growth of gurus is power—who has it and who is going to keep it. The question underlying each of these movements, be they psychological or religious, is: What are they doing to promote powerlessness among their followers, and what are they doing to abuse the gift of power? Too many times the goal of gurus is their own preservation; too many times the goal of the con-games of emotional growth is the perpetuation of the con.

Our position is: The goal of the guru should be you. The good teacher desires to free her students from their dependency; the good minister does not seek personal aggrandizement; the helpful psychological technique or interpretation or movement should consider self-destruction after a time.

Power, like the proverbial button, is hiding behind the facade of self-help, instant awareness, and quasi-religion. And the question is: Power? Power? Who has the Power?

Can the blind lead the blind? If so, where will they lead us, into more darkness or into real light?

> Once upon a time there lived a humble shepherd who quietly tended his flock of sheep, high upon a mountainside. The sheep grazed contentedly on good, green grass. And once a year the sheep gave the shepherd plenty of nice wool, with which he made himself a warm winter coat. The shepherd and his sheep were very happy together.
>
> Then one year the sheep learned of another flock who lived on a far away mountain, and who had overthrown their shepherd and taken control of themselves. Our flock decided self-government was a good idea, so they ran away from our humble shepherd. They went searching for their own mountainside and their own grass.
>
> The sheep walked in circles and squares for days, but they could find no grass as green as their home pasture. Soon, hungry and embarrassed, they went back to their humble shepherd. He was happy to see them and welcomed them home.
>
> But peace was not yet to be for our flock. A

second time the sheep followed one of their cousins, who had proclaimed the existence of a valley
of deep, deep grass, which was level and required
little climbing. However, soon the flock returned.
Disillusioned. They had found no valley.

Our story, regretfully, ends here. We cannot learn
the fate of our sheep. When we last see them, they
are grazing the mountainside. If there is a happy
or sad ending, we do not know it. Our story, we
fear, is a simple, perhaps confusing, story. It has
a beginning. There is no ending.

There are green grass and fences in all of our
lives. And there are questions too: Why do we
insist on believing in the perfect grass beyond
our fence? Why are our colors not bright enough?
And why can we not accept the humble shepherd
within ourselves?

Games and Gimmicks

Are you on a power trip, or are you tripping over
the power? Are you the puppet or the puppeteer?
Too many times, ends and means become confused. Too many times, the guru replaces you.

For example, the power of what we are
calling the con-games of emotional growth lies
not only in the leaders' desire for their own
growth, but in the techniques used. In too many
cases, the games of growth and the gimmicks of
brainwashing are similar. For your considera-
tion, we suggest a model which could be used in
personal warfare or welfare.

The following characteristics are found in
both brainwashing techniques and emotional
growth techniques:

Physical abuse
Significantly altering the physical
environment
The power of a central authority figure
Peer-group pressure
Swift reinforcement of desired behavior
Potential for an ongoing support system
High price

Physical abuse

For several years it has been "in" to equate pain with growth. Group marathon sessions are supposed to break down barriers between people; fatigue is supposed to allow the "real" you to emerge. A current group fad consists of two weekends in which participants are called "assholes" and "turkeys," are abused physically with marathon sessions in straight-backed chairs, are told to control their bladders, and told to clean up what they throw up. Another modality, following the theory of "no pain, no gain," realigns your body while inflicting great physical discomfort.

The list goes on; the assumptions are fantastic. Physical pain equals mental health. It is the castor oil school of psychology. It is a nazi-like school of therapy. We are suggesting that to abuse is to use, and the result is not personal freedom but indirect conformity and dependence.

Significantly altering the physical environment

Both religions and therapeutic groups have used the "retreat" technique. The idea has been to get "away" from the world in order to get more "into" the world. There is a "scream" therapy that demands that you leave your home environment and live near their centers, participating totally in their controlled environment. Growth centers are often isolated. The reason is simple. It is easier to gain complete control in home court. This control, we suggest, and this altering of environment is similar to traditional brainwashing techniques. There is a very fine line between systems which promote individual autonomy and personal conformity. It requires an acute perception and some courage to walk that line successfully. When the movement or technique or religion slips over that line into the promotion of conformity, it becomes bullshit, and should be avoided. Brainwashing is *not* emotional growth.

Central authority figure

Gods abound in the Emotional Growth Movement. Gurus bloom like the flowers of spring. People who are looking for answers are looking for *the someone* with those answers.

Every movement has its leader. There is a guru for you! There are leaders and followers, teachers and students. It is a dichotomy which does little to support personal autonomy.

Not only is the role of leader personalized by name, but it is also strengthened by act and ritual. The guru may be anonymous but his strength is unquestioned. The authority figure controls the meeting or session. He controls the environment. He controls.

Perhaps this mirror-like image of the con-games of emotional growth and brainwashing is by chance; perhaps it is by choice. The issue is irrelevant. What is relevant is the effect upon seekers of a controlling authority figure who seemingly is not human in that he has defeated the questions of life. He has the answers.

This guru position is set apart from human realities; he does not belch or fart; he does not have marriage or family problems; neither does he have a gnawing sense of inadequacy. He is above all that. He is authority and to accept this is to buy the con.

Peer-group pressure

Every group, by definition, sets norms of behavior. This sociological truth is sometimes forgotten in the huba-huba of personal growth.

In some groups there is pressure to confess one's sins loudly and to report. Remorse is stroked. The church has always loved a good sinner who would talk about his sins. In many groups depression is delightful and deliciously encouraged. One is supposed to acknowledge tension before having their body realigned. A participant in———is assumed not to have it and to want it. There is pressure in each group to be like all its members are and to be inadequate. The major assumption of the con-games is: You are not OK. The message is: You need us. So join and conform and you will be made well.

There is pressure on the person to accept the posture of the sick before the laying on of hands. Ministers love sinners; the doctor needs patients; the cop enjoys the existence of the crook. In plain language, the con-games of emotional growth encourage illness or not OK-ness. That is the paradoxical pressure of life and the Emotional Growth Movement.

Swift reinforcement of desired behavior

When you conform, you receive "strokes." Desired depression is stroked; warmth and enthusiasm get stroked; participating is stroking.

And stroking is sometimes literal in the Emotional Growth Movement. The big hug is the best of strokes. And the big hug can reinforce conforming behavior. Be like us and you will be hugged; refuse to conform and you will stand alone. That is the message of the B.S. movements and the concentration camp instructions. Nowhere was reinforcement so swift as in the concentration camp, or is so swift as in prison. That big hug can lead you into the prison of dependency. Beware the techniques of "desired behavior."

On-going support

Astro-travel groups offer free follow-up or refresher courses; you are a student of "scream" therapy for life; pseudo psycho-religious groups will reduce the rates the longer you are theirs; once a meditator, always counted as a meditator. Having joined the in-group, you are now *In*. The church or the Emotional Growth Movement offers a sense of significance to its communicants. The message is: You are now one of us. You are now special. That is a nice feeling, and to be encouraged. Yet television advertising sells the same feeling to users of Brand X or drivers of automobile Y. It is the effect of "the sell" that they are selling. Security is *in;* Individuality is *out.* When God spoke he talked of being with us always; when the gods of emotional growth speak, they talk of being with us always. God forbid!

High price

There is something in our cultural character which associates price and value. High cost/ good value. Cadillacs over Fords any day. This translates in the psychological marketplace: The higher the cost, the more therapeutic. The metaphysical therapy at $6,000 becomes the Cadillac of therapy. Another program costs $250 for two weekends; a consumer can spend thousands in "getting clear" or "finding the flow." Thus the Emotional Growth Movement is competitive, price wise, in the marketplace. And to be competitive is to imply value.

Again the ultimate question is: Who has the power? Are you looking for a flashlight salesman or are you groping in the dark for yourself? Are you susceptible to the games and gimmicks of those who would lead you unto them, or are you seeking power over yourself? Finally, can you see the issues of power behind the process of personal growth?

Again the question: Who is going to be the guru for you?

5

Products:

Psycho-Mumbo-Jumbo

A few years ago some folks found some yellow rocks in the streams of California. They called those rocks "gold." And the rush was on. California became the place of dreams; your local jeweler offered a technology; Omaha, Paola, Smithville or where-you-livedville became dullsville. There was gold in them thar hills! "Turn the horses west, Martha, we're goin' after gold."

The gold rush of the nineteenth century put California on the dream map, and altered the consciousness of an entire continent. But the last twenty years has seen a growth rush which, in numbers and dollars, makes gold seem worthless by comparison. Martha and Zeb are no longer going west for gold; they are headed north, east, south and west for personal growth. "Turn around, Zeb, you're on a one-way street."

Growth is gold. But before you rush to the pantry for your pans, listen.

Panning the streams of the mind is now Big

Business. Growth has incorporated. Forget the image of the solitary person living beside the cold-running stream, hoping against hope for a strike. That picture is historical myth. Now Bob and Carol and Ted and Alice have formed a consulting firm: Bob and Associates. Their advice is simple: Sell franchises. Be fruitful and multiply. Bonzo begat Son of Bonzo which begat the Return of Bonzo which also begat. We are a nation of begatters. Psychology has bought the hamburger model—growth in every town, on each corner. "Franchise!" advises Bob and Associates. "Grow."

What we now have in this country is a reverse rush. The streams are flowing to the seekers. California is coming to your town. The Emotional Growth franchise is coming to your door. Big Business is after the gold in your hills.

We are a far cry from the mythical Dr. Freud or that apparition called a wagon train. The last half of the twentieth century is observing a phenomenon which diminishes by comparison the movements of history—the mushroom growth of Emotional Growth. Personal growth has entered the board room, has incorporated, enfranchised, has gone after the gold. Simply put, industrial America has given birth to a growth industry. And Big Business is after Big Bucks!

The bottom line of business is black or red. No longer is the important question: Were you helped? Now the questions become economical. How many attended? Did we make a profit? What are the numbers?

When seen from this perspective, the industry of emotional growth produces products (courses, magazines, games, techniques, and gimmicks) which are to be sold to consumers. Thus, personal growth becomes a product for which a need must be created. Emotional growth joins the soap powders, detergents, and hair creams on the shelf at your local quick-stop store. And you are transformed into a consumer. That's it, Jack! That's it, Jill! You want mustard on your dog?

None of this is to imply that the emotional growth industry is not doing good. In fact, one of the philosophies of industry is: Large numbers mean good products. Or, as the salesman says, "You can't sell ice cream to Eskimos." We simply think you ought to see the package and what's inside before you buy. This book is consumer education. And those who spoke Latin years ago said it most concisely—*caveat emptor* (let the buyer beware).

However, no matter your A.Q. (Awareness Quotient), the psychology franchise, like the California stream, is selling a dream—self-improvement. And there is a market for this product in this society.

Advantage is often taken of the folk wisdom. On our good Mama's knees we learned that you don't get somethin' for nothin.' This pearl of wisdom translated: You get what you pay for. And this has led us to a belief in Cadillacs. Americans believe that the more money they spend the better product they buy. Therefore, the Cadillac is the best car because it is the most expensive. Right? Wrong! Using this logic, the bigger woman would make the best wife. A five thousand dollar diamond will drive a nail better than a two dollar hammer. No, the Cadillac wisdom of America is not right, but it exists nevertheless. What's wrong with big business, asks the patriotic echo? That depends, is the answer.

In psychology, price and competency have no direct correlation. The $60 analyst may be no better or worse than some across-the-fence advisor. The $35 per hour psychologist may be competent or incompetent. And the $250 weekend course in awareness may be a turn-on or a rip-off. Price is an economic bottom line. Competency or usefulness is a personal judgment, and is caught up more in the dream than in the streams.

We suggest to you that there is no such thing as a psychological quick-trip store. Franchising B.S. does not change the quality of the product; it simply allows it to spread and to be diluted still further. No single course, technique, or therapy can solve all of your problems. We don't believe in one-stop shopping. And in the darkest of your nights, just because the store is open for business doesn't directly translate into mellow evenings. Dark is dark, Jack and Jill. That's what being human is all about. That Cadillac you bought didn't solve all your problems and give you instant happiness, did it? Well, then why do you expect instant "growth" or "cure" from psychology?

What are the hidden costs behind the dollar signs? There are hidden costs in everything, Jill. Our Mamas told us that, too. What is the real price of the Cadillac? And what is the real price of the $250 course in emotional growth? What is the dependency factor? (The diabetic needs insulin every day. Will you need another course and another?) What is the rip-off factor? Are you being conned or cared for?

Finally, we are hoping that when you consider the consumption of self-help psychologies, you will be aware that they are, in many cases, big business after big bucks and possibly they may be B.S.

That's it, Jack. That's it, Jill.

But not quite.

Converting Trash into Cash

A casual glance at your local bookstore's psychology section will imprint two important facts. First, mental health is growing. Your bookseller, if shrewd, will rearrange his shelves to enlarge "Psychology" and make it more accessible to the grasping consumer. Martha, a friend I talked to at a party recently, said, "Americans have always been trendy . . . from hoola hoops to pierced ears . . . we are always trying to get on the band wagon." Hoola hoops are gone; mental health is here!

A second fact which holds the eye is all the junk titles in the psychology section. Titles, titles, and more titles. Our mind boggles at the number of self-help books or do-it-yourself-therapy titles, such as: *How to Be Your Best Friend, How to Read a Person Like a Novel, How to Be Awake and Aware, How to Get Close,* and *How to Be Happy and Healthy.* "How-to" books have been the backbone of the American book business for years. Now Martha, the housewife, wants to learn how to fix her life like she does her curtains, quilts, or plumbing. We live in the Solution Age, where for $1.95 plus tax the reader can find a solution for her life. Reading a book is the next best thing to "instant" cure. We'll take our therapies like our cocoa and coffee, and thank you very much.

The eye sees, but the mind cannot surround the boundaries of the possible: *How to Be Your Best Friend* fathers *How to Be Your Best Friend's Best Friend, How to Be Your Best Friend in Time of Crisis,* and shorter cousins *How to Be* and *How to Be Your Friend. How to Be Awake and Aware* marries *How to Be Happy and Healthy* and they begat that genetic giant *How to Be Happy and Alive and Aware and Healthy.* And he, if books become human, fathers human trapezoids in print form.

It is a publicist's dream. People devouring books which even hint at human betterment. Louis XIV must have been thinking of the "How-to" flood when he said, "After me, the deluge."

What are the limits? Who cries stop? Emotional growth is not sent down from the mountains to Matthew, Mark, and Luke. It is published from the thirty-seventh floor—which is to say simply, there are books which can help, and there are books which only help the pocket-books of the vice presidents in charge of merchandising.

What will tomorrow bring? *Therapeutic Quilting?* The eye can see the best sellers entitled: *Your Curtains and You, Self and Slip Covers, Plumbing Your Depths.* And the mind balks at *How to Be and Bees* and *How to Raise Earthworms for Profit and Self-Discovery.* The boundaries of the possible exist only in the minds of the psychological hucksters and the gullibility of the suffering, yet trendy, consumer.

While complaining to schools that little Johnny can't read, Johnny's mother and father are raiding the book shelves for child-rearing guidance. Or, perhaps Johnny can read what his desire for self-improvement leads him to. And don't forget that if it can be written, it can be merchandised. Soon there could be cassette courses in "Scream" therapy, Total Enlightenment for Non-Readers, and How to Be Your Own Psychiatrist in ten easy lessons. Remember: If it can be merchandised, it can be shortened, sweetened, made new and improved, put in pill form, discounted for fire and going-out-of-business sales, and in all ways made ready to be consumed.

The flood of self-help does not stop with books. There are lotions with which to massage your weary limbs as you listen to a stereophonic lecture on mind control. There are lotions to improve your marriage, lotions to stimulate your sex life, lotions which will make you a better lover, lotions for the feet, neck, sensory zones, and sensual stimulations. Rub your cares away; massage your worries. Your body is you, and as the jingle says, "You deserve a break today."

We agree with the philosophy. Your body is part of you. But it does not necessarily follow that you can be improved as a person with a body massage. In this message of the massage, there are hints of primitive exorcism and healing. The fundamentalist preacher laid on the hands in order for you to get closer to God. His hands cast out sin! And the man of God cleansed souls and cast out devils through the touch of his fingers. The soft hands of God are for reaching for your soul. Our creative vice president is no doubt already preparing "Soul Lotion," which, if gargled, massaged gently into temples or swallowed before every meal will "plug you into a greater awareness." Remember the name: "Soul Lotion."

What are the possibilities? Mr. Movie Star looking straight into the camera with his "I'm-a-good-guy-so-please-believe-me" smile and saying, "Early in my career I was going nowhere. I wasn't getting any parts. My wife ran off with an encyclopedia salesman. My kids were O.D.ing on Fritos. I was nowhere. Then a friend suggested I try "Soul Lotion" and, by golly, it changed my life. After just two weeks of "Soul Lotion," I was a new man. My wife came back to me. I got the lead in a great movie called "The Titanic Revisited" and my kids are on potato chips now. My life is complete, and I owe it all to "Soul Lotion."

"Cut."

"Print."

Or: Soul Lotion Tennis and Golf Tournaments. Prime time spots. New-Improved Soul Lotion. Extra-Dry Soul Lotion. For kids. For the family pet. For your love life!

Secret potion lotions . . . mysterious elixir . . . good for you!

If you can't read it, rub it on; if you can't rub it on, play it. Self-help games are the newest gimmicks of the industry. "Body Touch" allows the players to "plug in" to each other's body language; "Black-White" purports to improve empathy between races. There are games to improve listening skills, to reduce tension and relieve anxiety, to foster better communication problems, to improve marriages, to get a divorce, to . . .

The mind reels as the shadows grow. Competition becomes therapy:

> Welcome to the Therapy Game where contestants see who can dream the best Freudian nightmare. One point is scored for a simple sexual fantasy, two points for an oedipal conflict and a giant 1,000 points if you really try to kill your mother!

The guru look-alike contest on TV! Animated meditation for the kiddies. Transactional Soap Powder sponsors the Child-Adult game. The concept of Meditation Competition widens the world of sports. ABC Sports interviews the quarterback of the Sensitivity Team. The thirty-seventh floor reaches for our minds: The motto sells: "To compete is to improve. It pays to play."

Finally, probably the fastest growing segment of the human potential deluge is the greeting card industry. Self-awareness and pop psychology have become the staple in the belly button of the greeting card trade. This phenomenon is inter-disciplinary in that bad poetry has been added to simplistic or easy-answer psych to make mountains of millions for card and printer distributors. If Fritz Perls had foreseen the merchandising future of his Gestalt Prayer, he would have quit and gone to work for Hallmark. When Denise Levertov tires of serious poetry, her throw-aways might look wonderful as a message to a sick friend.

Every adolescent is a poster freak. No teen-

age bedroom is complete without rock stars star-
ing from the walls, and at least one "super-
saying." The teenager's mother has her favorite
psych-poem magnetized on the refrigerator and
her father has his epigram under glass on his
desk. Grandma sends Barry Boredom's poem
"You" to her friends, and Grandpa quotes pearls
of wisdom to anyone within earshot. The entire
American family is looking for the Quik-Trip
Store of Emotional Growth.

Cards, if they are to sell, can no longer contain impersonal messages suggesting inanities
like:

> Roses are red
> Violets are blue
> I like peanut butter
> Can you swim?
> Happy Birthday!

Terrible. But is the replacement much better.
Now "feelings" are paramount; "sensitivity" is
in:

> The sun lights my heart
> When I am with you.
>
> Your smile follows my shadow
> I feel good knowing you are with me.
>
> I am afraid
> When you are gone.

Oh, vulnerability reigns! Thin-skinned is in.
"Openness" becomes the criterion for good. The
bottom line is simple: Self sells.

We live in the interface of disciplines. Like
Godzilla and Frankenstein, advertising meets
psychology. Poetry grows on Madison Avenue.

Soap powders find Soul. Television finds the Human Potential Movement. Lotion cure! Books become therapeutic and greeting cards become the descriptive literature of an age. It is mind boggling and mind expanding. We are aware. And awareness sells.

6

Words:

B.S.,
Big Business,
and Big Bucks

We live in the land of the word. And we live in the land of illusion. Here in this place of verdant verbiage, words are real and words are illusion. People become plants and grow in direct proportion to vocabularies.

A few years ago a psychologist, Benjamin Whorf, suggested that our language forms the boundaries of our perception. If we have the word, we have the picture. Words become our reality. Our language is us.

Advertising shapes our desires through the word. Desires become needs. Needs are shaped then served by the word images which surround our lives.

Used car salesmen now satisfy our transportation needs. TV sets are transformed into home entertainment centers. Real estate people are out to help with our housing needs. Perhaps they are fulfilling needs, yet few stop to analyze the creation of needs. Words create needs which words then fulfill. We are used and abused by our own language.

We live in the wonderful world of Whorf. There is reality, and there is illusion, and there is our language which houses both illusion and reality. From the most miserable of truck stops to the best restaurants, the word "Eat" is all-encompassing; from Wall Street to Main Street, the words "Buy-Sell-Trade" are self-explanatory and suffer universal approbation. We live in a world which has given up on distinguishing between reality and illusion. Our common denominator is word.

Prolixity has become a virtue in psychology, as it has in literature, science, or art. Macrologic man reigns, if not superior, at least, from the top. Sesquipedalianism is equated with brilliance, intelligence, or good scholarship. Pleonastic prolixity has opened the door in the psychological world for the word *huckster*—the quack who wishes to camouflage both ends and means.

The Emotional Growth Movement, and many of its multipartite components, suffers not only from a terrible garrulousness but from the cultural confusion which confuses perception and illusion and which, therefore, while seeking to heal actually creates the need for healing. Well-meaning it is; beneficent it is not.

A humanistic jargon rules this world view. "Personal growth" becomes the litany of the psychologic service. People are broken down into "OK" parts; "Awareness" is the goal.

Within this context lie the myriad manifestations of the language and healing of human potential. Diversity is the commonality shared by the parts, yet their language reverberates in

similar fashion, pellucidity being not the goal.
The consumer is confronted with a vernacular
gobbledegook which, while purporting to heal,
serves best obfuscation. For example, in one
"pop" psychology brochure the author writes,
"Obviously the truth is what's so. Not so
obviously, it's also so what." He then asks
humanely and rhetorically, "Got it?"

As one confronts the argot of growth and
awareness, one is pressed to ask, "On whom is
the joke?" The phraseology may be short and
sweet, but it is not hard to beat! Here are some
examples:

"Hidden agenda"
"No strain, no pain"
"Balance body energy"
"Read the body"
"Here and now"
"Call For"
"Helps bring balance and order to the
energy flow"
"OK"
"Getting it"

*The language of human potential reflects the
paradox of much of our society: What was
designed to clarify actually adds to confusion.
The individual, confused, in pain, doubting, is
given paradoxical slogans as help. He or she
deserves better.*

But the beat goes on. If music were added, the
language of pseudo-religious and trendy psychologies would make a medieval chant of monk-
ish proportions.

Recognize/assert yourself/seek enlighten-
ment/awareness/flow/awaken/transform your
life/achieve/structural integration/find effective sensory perception/get into cosmic con-
sciousness/become a perfectly realized human
being.

And, like the monks of old, the bottom line of
the litany is for the believer to: *get it, lose it, find
it, clear it.*

The bottom line is to fit the person to the religion or psychology—and that is where it fails.
When understanding the words becomes the goal,
rather than understanding people, then psychology and religion have joined the paradox. When
you are asked to come to the system, you lose.

Benjamin Whorf's monster is alive and well
and living in the Emotional Growth Movement.
Words have become reality.

It is our suggestion that not only has the
language of "growth" become real, it has become meaningless as well. Energy, awareness,
growth, flow, assertion, effective sensory perception, enlightenment, and thousands of others
are words which, at a specific time and place,
might have had particular meanings, but now
they have been expanded to the boundaries of
meaninglessness. Words become garbage cans
into which are discarded meanings, possibilities, and future directions. The paradox of our
language and culture arises again! The more we
try to make our words mean, the less they mean.
Thus, the language of human potential, and much
of the religious verbosity, has become a con-
tainer for every human inflection, emotion, and
thought, and the more it contains, the less it

means. As *awareness* grows into multiple meanings, it grows less precise and, therefore, filled with less meaning. As *awareness* grows, *awareness* diminishes. Let us hope that as awareness grows, our awareness of growth will grow. Get it?

Traditionally, psychology has been imprisoned by the psychoanalytic language of illness. Oedipus was depressed by the situation with his mother, so he repressed those feelings of guilt, dreamed of sexual release and associated his dream with that time in early childhood when he couldn't urinate on a rose. Sheila, Oedipus' girlfriend, was drinking too much because her father once worked as a fireman. She projects her hatred of her mother onto Oedipus and demands that he wear a skirt, an apron, and stay in the kitchen. Oedipus and Sheila marry and live unhappily ever after.

Diagnosis: Oedipus is sick.

Diagnosis: Sheila is sick.

Diagnosis: The language of psychoanalysis may be sick.

Prescription: A language of health.

Now, Oedipus is not sick, he has joined an encounter group where he is "confronting" his problems; he is becoming more "aware," is "growing"; he is becoming "sensitized" to his situation.

Sheila is learning to "communicate" her anger; she is learning to "assert" herself. She "gets in touch" with her feelings toward Oedipus. Some possible results are:

Scenario No. 1: Sheila "decides" marriage is for the birds; she wants to be "free."

Scenario No. 2: Oedipus and Sheila marry, but
see marriage not as roses and lollipops, but as a
continuing effort at "communication." Both are
"aware."

Scenario No. 3: (The authors invite the readers to
write their own.)

Health is vocabulary. We changed from a
model of sickness to a model of health switching
vocabularies. What you say is what you pay. Yet,
no matter how you say it, you still have to pay it.
The words of health have their own sickness.

Martha: I've been feeling depressed lately.
Jane: It depresses me to hear that you've been
feeling depressed.
Martha: Oh, it makes me feel good to know that
my depression depresses you.
Jane: And I feel good about your feeling good.

"I'm aware of my anger towards you."

"I have been aware of your anger for some
time now."

"Well, I'm aware that you've been aware of
my anger, and now I'm aware of even more anger
towards you because you didn't do anything
about your awareness of my anger."

"In this group we are going to become sensitized to our sensual selves."

"That's a crummy idea. It doesn't touch me at
all."

"Why are you crawling around on the floor
like that?"

"I'm getting in touch with my primal feelings."

"Aw shit! That's so stupid!"

"You mean you don't understand why I'm
doing this?"

"I mean I think what you are doing is a lot of shit!"

"Well, (standing up) I want to tell you that I think you are a narrow-minded son-of-a-bitch because you can't see the importance of what I'm doing."

"And I think you are a pansy and too fagish to be a real man."

"Here. Get in touch with the skin of my fist."

"I feel very good."

"I feel very good too."

"Does that mean we both feel very good?"

"No, it means we both have said we feel very good."

P.S. Jumbo was an elephant. Mumbo was a frog. Psycho was their son by marriage. His full name was Psycho-Mumbo-Jumbo. And he was a good/bad boy who flew/walked through life/death doing good/bad deeds, slaying mon/mansters and saving/drowning maidens. Finally Psycho-Mumbo-Jumbo went on a great voyage to Never-Never Land. He found Never-Never Land full of perspicacious paradox, which fitted Psycho-Mumbo-Jumbo perfectly. So Psycho-Mumbo-Jumbo decided to stay in Never-Never Land. He lives there still.

7

Sex:

Play Now,
Pay Later

Have you ever wanted to walk naked through the park, or down the streets?

Are you tired of your life? Would you like to "make it" with someone not your spouse and not have to feel guilty about your "affair"?

How would you like to hold an attractive stranger in your arms?

Improve your sex life!

Be a better lover!

Sexual awareness! Feeling therapy!

Is there a hint of mystery for you in the phrase "sexual awareness"?

Does "touchy-feely" sound good to you?

The "growth" industry is filled with sexual come-ons and innuendos. We might say our cups runneth over!

The implied messages of many courses,

groups or techniques, is that you will be a "new, improved lover" after they are through with you. It is the old Charles Atlas game applied to sexuality: Before you were a 90 pound weakling who, before the Sandman kicked sand in your face, said "Not tonight, dear, I'm too tired." But after a weekend of _____, there is a tiger in your tank. Muscles bulge! You become a marathon lover—satisfying to all. Millions of young boys, hungry for manhood, bought the Charles Atlas muscle-building course, practiced religiously, then went to the beach hoping some bully would even look cross-eyed at them. Whammo! And they were sure to get the girl too.

Well, as we males know, reality didn't quite measure up to our dreams. We either bought the muscle-building course, practiced and then some bully still beat the hell out of us and stole our girl, or we bought the course but then forgot to practice our muscle-building routines and were, therefore, still scared of the beach bullies, or, we just grew older with our fears and our hunger for manhood until we finally realized that muscles and manhood really had little in common.

Just as the Charles Atlas muscle-building course was selling us an image of ourselves which was, perhaps, possible, but not probable, the sexual innuendo of the growth industry suggests as possible what we, in our deepest hearts, desire. Every husband wishes to sexually satisfy his wife. Each woman wants to make her man happy. Aren't both of them nervous on that first night together? Aren't both of them searching for reassurance about their ability to sexually satisfy?

And that is where the sexual come-on of "growth" comes in. First, they create the expectation of more or better. Do you mean you and your wife don't do it standing on your heads? Have you experimented with the fireman's carry or fisherman's way? Do you mean to say that you are still using the old missionary approach to sex? Horrors! The implied message is clear: What you are is not OK. If you could be freed from your old inhibitions, you could become more sexually aware. Your husband has tolerated you for twenty years, but just think what you could do for him if you were to become a new sexual you!

The first step is to create dissatisfaction with what is. Then, the second step is to offer high expectations for what might be. This is the sales approach that works with detergents, automobiles, muscles, and sex. It is the old carny shell game applied to growth psychology.

So the mark, oops, rather the consumer, takes the course, reads the book, attends the meeting, and so on, expecting to find the solution to his or her sexual dissatisfaction. And, sometimes we find what we expect to find. But not often. Once in a while the carny must let a mark win; there are winners in Las Vegas, but Vegas is the big winner; a few boys become men through the Charles Atlas muscle-building course, but most do not.

When you play, you pay. There ain't no free lunch, baby! And that is the lesson which the sexual come-on goes against. Sexual awareness is simply too simple an answer for the complex problems of being human. Also, it disregards the price tag on intimacy. When people get close, there is a price to pay. The human psyche does not only live in the present; it contains the past and future and present. So play now, pay later might be the appropriate phrase. For example, when John and Mary meet in the group, each is bringing a total past with them; although they might like to forget wives, husbands, kids, lovers, or families, it doesn't work that way. Memory is our saving faculty and our burden. And no matter what happens between them here, each will remember and have to cope with those memories. Perhaps, in the name of "growth," there will be fine sex between them. Still the question remains: Will Mary feel guilty later? Will John feel like he took advantage of her? Will one or both regret the actions of yesterday tomorrow? If the answer to any of these questions is "Yes," then the price is too high.

Our complaint with parts of the Emotional Growth Movement is that they use sexual innuendo, the promise of sexual improvement, as a come-on to attract you, with seemingly little regard for the complexity of sexual function or the human mind. There are those of us who are suffering greatly with sexual dissatisfaction. And to them "growth" psychology offers a disservice when it provides emotional Band-Aids and con-games of simplicity. *Play now, pay later* is inflexible as a law of human life. It must be dealt with by the answers in our lives.

Interpersonal does not mean intercourse. Our sex lives are important, but they are just one thread in the fabric of humanness. Better in bed does not necessarily lead to being a better person. Having an affair, legitimized by psychology or not, may not improve your marriage. In fact, the odds are against it. Interpersonal is a word which signifies all that goes on between two people; it is an all-inclusive word. It includes all verbal and nonverbal behavior. Interpersonal implies the totality of human experience, and when certain books or groups suggest the close correlation between interpersonal and intercourse, implying the improvement of one equals an improvement in the other, they are not only just B.S.ing the consumer, they are harmful.

No book or course or weekend can supply the answer for your sex life. Current research is suggesting that books or courses can help people in crisis *if* they come at the right moment in the crisis. But here we aren't just talking about crisis situations; we are talking about that most intimate of acts between two people. And no book or therapy can replace a person in your bed.

An improved sex life is not *the answer* to all your problems. We know of couples who have had a sustaining and nurturing marriage, which included a so-so or even unhappy sex life. And there are those folks who are tigers in bed but who just can't make it as a partner the other twenty-three hours of the day. Sex is one part of a total relationship, and it may or may not be an important part for you. But even if it is important, there is little correlation between improving sex and improving you.

The con-artists who offer intercourse as the equivalent to interpersonal are selling band-aids as a cure for deep wounds. Sex sells. Everyone knows that. We sell automobiles, vacations, refrigerators, anything, with sexual innuendos. A pretty girl in a bikini and a hog farm equals your dream vacation. Sex does sell. But it sells simplistically, and, perhaps, harmfully. There ain't no such thing as a quik-trip orgasm store for eternal happiness!

Emotional Rape

Sigmund Freud was right: Too many of us *are* sexually repressed. Perhaps as a culture we handle our sexuality very poorly. But we are as ambivalent about sex as we are about other parts of our cultural personality. We wish to free ourselves, yet we are afraid of the results. We choose to remain comfortable in our pain.

Elmer Gantry was right: Seduction and conversion are strongly linked. If memory serves correctly, Elmer Gantry, the revivalist preacher who travels from town to town to convert the nonbelieving, rationalizes his desire for the young ladies of the town by suggesting that it is his duty to lead the young ladies to religion, and that every seduction is a conversion.

Freud was right: We are preoccupied with sex; Elmer Gantry was right: Seduction and conversion are closely linked desires. And the con-games of emotional growth use both models to attract adherents. Sigmund Freud and Elmer Gantry may make strange bedfellows, but the bottom line is an effective come-on. What the consumer pays for when he buys into the B.S. games of emotional growth may have more to do with one's sexual fantasies than one's realities.

Sexual repression or a feeling of sexual inadequacy *is* an important piece in our cultural puzzle, and we are not suggesting that sexual function, therefore, is not a legitimate area of concern for psychology and religion. If these disciplines are to be relevant, they must be concerned with the problems of the people. However, when a sexual innuendo is used to advertise personal growth, the Emotional Growth Movement deserts its own goals and becomes not only extraneous but, perhaps, harmful. The line between bullshit and better is fine indeed.

This story happens too often. Betty, age thirty-six, recently divorced, lonely, emotionally drained and confused responded to a course or group which offered "heightened awareness" or "sensory awareness." During the course, Betty was attracted to Rick, another participant. And given an emotional environment in the group which encouraged letting all emotions "hang out" and "freeing up," Betty and Rick had sexual intercourse. They both enjoyed the experience and the group. Later, however, after the course had ended, Betty and Rick went their separate ways, and Betty began to feel a sense of guilt about having sexual intercourse with a man she hardly knew. So now not only was Betty divorced, alone and confused, she was also feeling guilty about her actions. The course not only had not helped, it had actually been harmful.

It could be said that the Emotional Growth Movement is not responsible for the consumer's feelings, just as any teacher is absolved from blame for her student's future actions. However, we are suggesting that the courses and techniques which desire to be helpful must consider all of the possible consequences, and educate its adherents about them. Furthermore, when it is irresponsibly implied that sexual arousal is necessarily therapeutic, emotional growth has adapted the Elmer Gantry model.

Our fictitious story has a counterpart in reality every day. People pay for growth and receive sex. If sex is synonymous with growth, then every massage parlor is a growth center, every prostitute a therapist. We are not suggesting that every part of the Emotional Growth Movement uses sex as either a come-on or an explicit goal, but we are suggesting that those parts that do, risk simplifying both personal growth and the sex act. And when simplification occurs, the consumer ought to wear high boots.

Sexual intercourse is a complex subject which utilizes the emotional states of people. When these people are already made emotionally vulnerable, to even suggest sexual intercourse as a therapy would be to play with emotional fires. Personal growth is also a complicated process which is desired, but little understood. To simplify this process by equating growth and sex is a disservice to human knowledge, as well as a personal violation. At what price do we simplify both sex and personal growth?

Interpersonal does not mean intercourse!

There is a difference between a massage and a message!

Growth and sex are not synonymous!

Elmer Gantry and Sigmund Freud are strange bedfellows!

8

Dangers:
Growth Addiction

Too many parts of the Emotional Growth Movement or the new and old pseudo-religions actually diminish rather than enhance people's lives. If the starting assumption of any program or idea is that its consumer or constituent is not OK, then what you have is a hospital. It is the medical model reinvigorated.

The traditional medical model of relationship assumes that:

There is a patient who is in need of cure/help.
There is an authority who will analyze/diagnose the problem and prescribe a cure.
The patient will be thankful (implicit).
The patient will come to depend on the authority and will legitimize the source of that authority (implicit).

A paradox of living is:

> Cures create illnesses.
> Supply creates demand.
> A hamburger stand creates hamburger eaters.
> The Growth movement creates its own groupies.
> Emotional growth helps create those in need.

Doctors create patients. Hospital beds exist to be filled. Insurance companies create people who need insurance. And psychoanalytic psychology perpetuated the medical model by creating an unconscious part of people that could only be analyzed/understood by the analyst—the authority.

The Emotional Growth Movement was ostensibly created to provide a viable alternative to the medical model of illness. Part of it may actually offer an alternative. But too many times what has been created has simply reinforced the dependency of the medical model. And the basic assumption, too many times, is: You, the consumer, the client, are not OK.

If this were a recipe for an Emotional Growth Cake, we would take this basic assumption of individual conflict, add one cup of good old fashioned religious dependency, add two-thirds of a cup of protestant/American work ethic, a teaspoonful of individualism and a gallon of "shoulds" and "should-nots." Again, if this were a pastry product, it would:

Create a sweet-toothed American
Suggest that it cures a sweet-tooth problem
Suggest that if you suffer from sweet-
tooth, then there must be something
wrong with you

And we would suggest that:

This cake should be labeled "May be
dangerous to the Health of the
Consumer."

As our Emotional Growth Cake grows, a
primary myth emerges:

"We will help you to be free. Just depend on us!"

Bullshit! Dependency is *not* freedom. Thus,
the course, religion or psychology, which shouts
"freedom" but encourages dependency has a
vested interest in encouraging failure.

Too many parts of the Emotional Growth
Movement seek long-term growth for themselves. Therefore, their implicit goals are to
create growth groupies. They wish to create a
sustaining audience which will consume any
group, idea, or methodology. Every self-named
guru is looking for students. Therefore, the bottom line is: To keep the consumer in perpetual
need, constantly dependent, and forever coming
back for more. Growth groupies are not just a by-
product of growth psychology, they are the goal.

Failure is encouraged when too-high expectations, or "shoulds," are shouldered by the con-

sumer. You *should* improve, "be clear," "get it," "find it," or "lose it" by meditating, taking our course, or joining this group. The vicious circle begins, and does not end. High expectations create built-in failure which, in turn, creates new expectations which create new failure.

So, although failure is not acceptable to the Emotional Growth Movement, it finds itself encouraging that which it proclaims to find uncomfortable. It is a double message, sent and received. The individual consumer is caught between the pushing and pulling of growth. The result is, at best, confusion. At its worst this system is actually destructive to the people it purports to help.

Another common myth which pervades the medical model and growth psychology is: Pain is growth. To struggle, to suffer is to grow. The person becomes better through pain.

Bullshit. This is just another way of saying, "Castor oil is good for you." The pain in growth psychology is Grandma's castor oil philosophy legitimized by authority. It is pure hokum! And it, too, can be destructive.

Scream therapy encourages pain as a way of "working through" your emotions; the body therapist twists and pummels your body to release tension and feelings. Modern exorcism? Psychology? Castor Oil? What is this philosophy that believes in physical pain, and suggests a correlation between physical pain and emotional growth? What are its ends? Where do we stop? Does a broken leg equal end of depression? Might a nice pulled muscle mean emotional release? Where does this end and where are we checking our brains when we buy this P.T. Barnum stuff? If we find pleasure in pain what does that say about us?

So, the B.S. of the movement is putting forth a disguised medical model, which implicitly asks: What is wrong with you? We have a pain killer creating a market of pain. And we have a castor oil philosophy of Grandma dressed up and portrayed as a psychological truth. What we have is a lot of myths whose factual basis is assumed and which are set out as psychological truths. Finally, we have B.S. groups, programs and books which are trying to imprison the consumer between its myths and its realities. A double-message creates double-talk and double-talk allows a double-vision. In the Emotional Growth Movement what you see is not always what you get. And what you get may diminish you as a person.

The Ultimate Fix

The promise of life, the hint of death. That is what we are searching for. The young look to drugs to take them our of the ordinary and beyond themselves. Marijuana mountains and Cocain high. A whole new language has been created around this seeking; a "joint has ceased to be perjorative and now holds far implications and great expectations; a "roach" is something to be desired; "gold" is to be smoked. New language, same meaning.

And the parents of the young, driven by their own fears and desires, taught that drugs were bad, alcohol was good. So our children wanting approval, quit smoking and took up the glass. Gold is old. Beer is here.

It is an ultimatum. There are thirteen-year-old alcoholics. Fourteen year old winos. The weekend date needs the bottle shared to be complete. It is the search they and we are addicted to. *And theirs is an ultimatum to us: Love us the way we are, because the way we are is the way we thought you wanted us to be.*

The search for the ultimate fix. That is what we share. And this commonality takes many forms: fundamental–I found it–religion, booze, work, pot, or the many answers of the Emotional Growth Movement. The dream is wide. We are searching for the promise of life.

As the description unfolds and our explanation of the lure of emotional growth evolves, the one common characteristic which the young and old, drinkers and smokers and meditators and all the true believers, share is that their searching is done with others. Do not leave me alone. We smoke together; drink together; get high together. We are, as paradoxical as it may seem, a togetherness people. The one moment we all fear is that sweep of the hand which finds us alone.

Do not leave me is our plea. Come with me is our supplication. Join me is a social law.

And the kind of dream that the emotional growth movement offers is "growth together." At that point it aligns itself with paradoxical us, tunes into some wave-length, becomes, in fact, part of us and ours. "Personal growth–together." Personal awareness–at the same time; individual exclamation as a collective voice. Irony has always escaped our minds, while becoming our reality.

Growth offers getting high with thousands by your side. In one weekend group there may be 250 you's out to "get it." A million meditators seek personal enlightenment as if they were astrologers counting stars to infinity. Group therapy, rationalized by cost, replaces the loneliness of one-to-one. Primal screams are heard by the hundreds, and emitted by more.

The growth movement speaks to its believers in simple words: You are not alone. The listener is massaged by those words. That is what we want to hear. There is safety in numbers (less risk). There is affirmation in numbers. (I am not *too* different). There is security in numbers. (We are in this together).

The varying movements need true believers, and true believers need each other. We search, yet our search takes us along common paths. We wish to find ourselves. The one most prominent, and, therefore, inescapable fact about our dream is that it is shared.

Our search for the Answer Man or for something or someone who can remove the doubting darkness from our lives has followed a logical pattern: Alcohol, drugs, religion, psychology. The new salesman has something to sell. The new priest is of this world, yet a purveyor on high.

The common thread of this progressive search is that all steps can be seen, perhaps should be seen, as drugs. Alcohol is a drug; marijuana is a drug; religion also; and growth too can be a synthetic dream. And when seen as a drug, growth or human potential psychology and its derivatives can be seen in its disillusioning forms as well. Not only can it produce great highs, but here is also a danger of addiction and overdose.

Not only has the last decade been a time for the growth of growth psychology, it has also seen the growth of the groupies of growth. Many are the people who travel from one guru to another, from body therapy to meditation to sensitivity training to sexual awareness, ad infinitum. Like little satellites around the stars, they seek new knowledge, new techniques, new awareness. They seek to find it, get it, lose it, get in touch with it, be aware of it. They take the course, find their problems unsolved or only partially so, then move on. They are the true believers, the children of the dream.

The groupies of growth are those veterans of the growth circuit who, having inculcated the language and ritual of growth, become professional seekers, perpetual growers. Their role is to find and initiate new students. Their function is to go about the land spreading a gospel of growth. Their definition is that of seeker or dreamer. Their fulfillment is found in the process of search. To find would be to hint at death; to quit believing would be death itself.

Every drug has a prescribed dosage. When this is exceeded, there is danger of overdose. And just as there are those who are addicted to growth, there are also those who suffer from too much growth. The man who ended up mortgaging his house to pay for his enlightenment course has overdosed. The graduate of an existentialist philosophy group who truly believes that our fate is in our hands, disparages the rest of us as weak-willed and, therefore, to be despised, is dead in a human way. The true believer who can only see the ritual in which he is engaged and misses the personal suffering and joy going on around him has been blinded by his attempt to see.

When one speaks of drugs, one must speak of glorious possibilities, inglorious addiction and dependency, the possibility of overdose, and the growth of true believers. Growth has become one of our miracle drugs. It holds a promise of life and a hint of death.

9

Overview:

Stepping Back to Look Foreward

We have tried to critically examine those assumptions which lie hidden behind the proliferating B.S. psychologies. Before we close, let's summarize what we have said:

- "Growth" psychology is suffering with diarrhea. New groups are born every day; new therapies are born at night.

- The symptoms of this cumulative dis-ease include confusion among consumers, emotional simplicity, therapy through language, ill-defined goals for those who are trying to help, enticing come-ons, outlandish and irresponsible claims, misunderstood assumptions, and sloppy "help."

- The result of this dis-ease has been the growth of the groupies of growth and the growth of the growth itself.

- The diarrhea of the Emotional Growth Movement continues today.

We have suggested that a close look at the assumptions of most books, courses, or techniques which comprise what we have called the Emotional Growth Movement, results in the conclusion that too much of it is destructive bullshit. And we have suggested that you, the consumer, ought to question carefully those B.S. assumptions. For example, you should not miss:

- That *power* is the central issue in many of these new helping fads—who has it and to what ends will it be used?

- That a *psycho-mumbo-jumbo* pervades the psychological marketplace, and often passes itself off as therapeutic.

- That *sex* sells psychology as well as automobiles.

- That *growth* is a garbage word that is relatively meaningless, and, therefore, can be used as an umbrella to cover all sorts of mischieviousness.

- That many components of the Emotional Growth Movement actually create problems by *encouraging weakness* in you.

- That "therapy" or "help" is now *big business* and therefore, the bottom line is often no longer you, but the dollar sign.

- That you, the reader and consumer, are part of the problem too. Since you insist on looking for easy answers, the Answer Man is born; since you insist that your life is not OK and could be better, there are those who are happy to feed on your expectations; since you insist on looking for your answers "out there," there are those who are happy to be your authorities; and since you insist on paying for quality, you are made to pay for its substitute as well.

Yes, your eyes are not deceiving you. The ultimate culprit in this scenario is you. This book would not have to be written if you had more faith in yourself, more trust in the totality of human experience, and less belief in the existence of the pie in the sky. But do not blame yourself too much. You are a paradoxical creature.

> While disbelieving in bargains, you search for something for nothing; while putting down the every-day psychologist, you reach out to every pseudo-psychologist and quack as he comes along; while dieting you eat; while living, you dream.

That paradoxical quality about you is both strength and weakness; it is exciting, and it frustrates both you and us. So we write this book hoping it will touch part of your life, will open your eyes to what they are doing to you and to what you are doing to yourself; we hope it will assist.

Help . . . I've Been Helped!

"Help" is another of those garbage words which populate our language, in general, and the psychological vernacular, in particular. Many people in many different professions see themselves as "helpers." But too few are the times when we stop to question what help really means and what helpers do. With the Emotional Growth Movement as our primary focus, let us, for a moment, take a look at the word and the professions that have grown up around it.

> Help . . . "to give assistance to" "to be of use to"
> Help . . ."a source of aid" (*Webster's Seventh New Collegiate Dictionary*)

To be of help is to offer assistance, to be a

source of aid. However, that definition does not go far enough. It fails to concern itself with a time span, the continuity of life. The questions remain: If you are a source of aid today, will you be so tomorrow? If I need your assistance now, will I continue to need help? In short, what is the goal of help? Is the goal to create a space for its continuing need, or is the goal self-help, where a person can come, ultimately, to be a source of aid for himself or herself?

These are the questions with which helpers and the helping professions must contend, and these are the questions which are at the heart of our struggle with what we have called the con-games of emotional growth.

To help you, your family doctor prescribed a drug which creates a dependency within you. Soon you will need help to free yourself from the helper.

Too many times psychiatrists reach for the pill bottle to treat children with emotional problems. The symptom is drugged; the problem remains.

As a society, we institutionalize those who do not fit in. The "crazy" are put in mental illness reservations. Criminals are imprisoned. This out of sight, out of mind philosophy is called help.

Koffee klatch advice is called help.

And, whether it be scream therapy, meditation, sensory awareness, mind control courses, or whatever, the many parts of the Emotional Growth Movement offer help as a product. The basic assumption is that there is consumer need for their help. The view of you is one of inadequacy, incompetence, using less of your potential, incomplete—in a word, helpless. You are helpless. You need their help. And, for the sake of argument, perhaps you do need help. But it is at this crucial point that the seminal questions arise: What does help mean? What is its goal? Will you be stronger or weaker after being helped? This is the crunch point.

It is our suggestion that, like other helping professions, in too many cases the growth movement's help only serves to weaken you. Although you have "got it" or are more "tuned in," "in touch with," or more "aware," in the long run you have been made less able to deal effectively with the rocks and arrows of life. Today you have group support. Tomorrow you will be alone again. The question remains: In your tomorrows will you be able to help yourself?

We contend that in too many cases (and one may be too many), growth psychology opens the can without any thought about protecting the contents against the consequences of can opening. A woman attends a course in awareness training (or any of dozens of others) and is made more sensitive to herself and the world around her. Then she goes home and is clobbered by an insensitive world. She is in great emotional pain, emotionally bleeding. She is confused. Has she been helped?

Sometimes the growth movement, with its litany of personal responsibility, growth, awareness of feelings, etc., is building glass houses. Its consumers are made more vulnerable to an uncaring world. A person can be emotionally undressed and, therefore, made susceptible to every nuance of the elements. We suggest that if in your tomorrows you are not stronger and less vulnerable to wind shifts, if your glass house is not reinforced, then you have been ripped off by the con-games of emotional growth. If techniques, schools of thought, or philosophies are going to ask you to change or "grow," then they have an obligation to emotionally support you while you are growing. Our bottom line for help is self-help. If I can help you to help yourself, then I have been of help. But if I want to help you so you will come to depend on me, then you have been conned.

We can become victims of help. An analogy is clear: Being helped is sometimes like being mugged and raped. After our bodies are manipulated, our emotions dissected, our heads filled with B.S. and our wallets emptied, do we report the act to the police or do we consider ourselves as having "grown"? The con-games of emotional growth do indeed rape us when and if they offer to help us without contending with the consequences of such an act. Sometimes we can be the victims of easy help.

Too many times we are forced to cry: "Help . . . I've just been helped!"

Please Don't Help

I can well remember when my father taught me how to ride my first bicycle. I shall not bother you with the details. However, I will report my feelings of anger and frustration when he continued holding on to me, as I wobbled along, after I felt I was in control. Dad had held me up as I learned to balance on two wheels, but because he wanted to protect me from harm, he held on even when I had ceased to need him. That was when I felt angry. I was ready to ride on my own! I wanted to be free of Dad's support. I wanted (although I was not then able to articulate this) to be the captain of my own two-wheeled ship.

Now, as a parent, I can understand the feelings of my father. I, too, wish to protect my child from harm. Yet already in this pre-bicycle stage I can see that my son has his "don't help" moments. He wants and needs those times when he can feel free of support, when he can stand alone.

The toughest job of a parent is to let go. And he must start practicing letting go in the first year, if not day, of a child's life. The paradox of parenthood, which makes the role extremely difficult, is that one must constantly and simultaneously practice holding on and letting go.

To not help may be more difficult a posture, yet more important, than to offer help. And, as we hope you understand by now, it is our contention that the goal of therapy, help or call-it-what-you-will should be self-determination. Just as a parent must be able to let go when the child demands it, the helping professions must discipline themselves to quit helping. And you, as a consumer of the human potential movement, must come to demand this letting go. We hope that you can come to see that your bottom line is you.

To arrive at this desired point, you must first come to see that you have a choice. When the con-games of emotional growth suggest that you are presently inadequate or not fulfilling your potential. you must see that you have a choice to believe or ignore them or you may choose to seek help, but that too must be seen as a choice.

If you are asking for help, you are choosing to do so. If you are rejecting offered assistance, you are choosing.

The bottom line of your life is the choices you make.

Throughout this book, our goal for you has been understated yet evident. We hope you can come to a point in your life when you can say to those who are offering assistance, and thereby refusing to let go, as we did to our fathers at bicycle time, "Please don't help . . . I don't need you anymore!" Anything less than this is B.S. And any course, technique, or movement whose game is not exactly this is a con-game of emotional growth.

We want to shout this, because we want to be sure you hear it:

> The bottom line is *you*!
> You can choose!
> Help is a choice you make!

Now at this point the autonomous reader should be shouting back: Shut up! I don't need you anymore!

If you are shouting back at us, then we are happy. We shall smile proudly as we watch you pedal down the street by yourself.

This is not to say that we are against any support or assistance. You may need help at this moment. If you do, we would hope you would make a knowledgable choice.

Help *should* be available if you want it. When asked for, emotional growth *should* be yours. Those are our two "shoulds," but they are far different than those with which you may be generally bombarded.

Obvious Observations

Unless you want to be taken for a ride to Rip-Off City, you must learn to defend yourself against the con-games of emotional growth. And the one prominent fact about the growth psychology consumer is that he is generally ill-prepared to evaluate new and proliferating programs. A Ph.D. would help only a little in trying to make sense of the products which deluge the consumer. Therefore, since this book was written for you, we take a moment here, as we have done throughout, to describe the weaknesses in the psychological marketplace, and to suggest certain parameters which might guide your actions.

If you are thinking of entering the Emotional Growth Movement market as a consumer, we suggest that you:

A. Stop.
B. Remember that *you* are your last line of defense.
C. Now, proceed with caution to:
  1. Identify your needs.
  2. Make clear what you expect to receive.
  3. Ask yourself: Does what is offered fit my value system?
  4. Examine your attitude toward the product, course or technique.

5. Try to see how the product fits into your view of yourself.
6. Ask yourself: Is this product offering the answer for my life, and am I looking for such an answer?

The foregoing is *not* a foolproof system. You might complete each step and still buy a one-way ticket to Rip-Off City. However, we think your chances of being conned will be reduced if you will consider carefully the messages of this book.

Secondly, although word-of-mouth is generally good advice and a filter which separates the rip-off and the turn-on, we would remind you that it is susceptible to the weaknesses already mentioned, namely: True believers are out spreading the good word; the true believers, in order to justify themselves, need to have you join them; there is a bandwagon effect which is at play in every movement; the name of the game for the Madison Avenue-type folk is the creation of need, thus the packaging of the product may be deceiving, making observation unreliable and judgment difficult; many products or movements are cloaked in the mystery of psychology itself. The false syllogism goes:

The mind is complex and mysterious;
_____ has to do with the mind;
Therefore, _____ is complex and mysterious,
and, therefore reputable.

The reasoning is as false as the product may be.

However, given the preceding qualifications, we suggest word-of-mouth as a place to begin. Just remember to take your salt pills before swallowing what you hear. In this individualized world wherein each of us is different and you are your own bottom line, what your friend or neighbor sees may not be what you get.

Thirdly, remember that Hitler had good references too. Those who wanted to believe in him, believed in him. If old Adolf had been selling awareness training, the consumers would have lined up to partake of his wares. He came highly recommended. And when he arrived, he was a surprise.

All this is to say that before buying into the Emotional Growth Movement, you might inquire about the leader, ask to see or hear his qualifications, references, ask about his goals or objectives for the course or technique he is offering. Find out what his bottom line is.

Finally, a small rule of thumb which you might use to quickly separate the rip-off and the turn-on is: Will the leader describe what you will be asked to do before you enroll? Now no leader will wish to fully describe every nook and cranny. Asking him to do this will make him feel like you are after something for nothing. Yet, every potential consumer has a right to a general outline, sufficient to make a decision. And if the public relations person or the leader refuses such an outline and claims mystery, you can be sure he is a B.S.er. If the work is secret, you don't want any part of it. If the bottom line is hidden, forget it.

Postscript:

P.S. No More B.S.

The last decade has seen the growth of garbage and gurus. The emotional growth industry is a big business and fast growing. Since 1960 self-improvement, examination, and, even in certain time and place, immolation have been cultural mottos, if not natural goals. What has become a movement began in earnest as a dedicated few searched for new perspectives. Freud had to be buried. Man had failed to resolve deeper issues of self-degradation. But as with most social phenomena, what began in search evolved into litany (when God became silent, the church began to sing). This took various forms, expanded, and was transformed by those it attracted. A snowball rolled across the psychological landscape picking up dirt and snow alike. P.T. Barnum therapists, quick-buck artists, and "helpers" of all persuasions were drawn to emotional growth, and because they came, it was different. Growth became a garbage word, meaningless to most, yet still an umbrella of vast proportions. Emo-

101

tional growth became, in too many cases, a brand name which legitimized the can. And the can was the package for the con.

It is a time of retrenchment. We must look back in order to go forward. This book tries to apply an unusual but powerful standard to the proliferating games of growth, namely: common sense and sanity. This book is a crap detector. We present it to you. Use it in good health. This is a book whose time has come.

And the message? Simple. The con-games of emotional growth either disregard, are insensitive to, or hide the real issue behind self-improvement, which is power. Like the proverbial button, who has the power is the question. And this issue of power, like love, both attracts and repels us.

We are afraid of power. We worship its mystic. It is a goal and to be avoided. The paradox of power reflects the contradictions of our lives.

The main issue in emotional growth is power. Who is going to be in charge of your life? What authority says the grass is greener beyond the fence? Who is your final authority?

Yet, power is real and fantastical: Does the Lone Ranger still ride into your life? Will silver bullets solve your problems? Why do we have a sense of fear as we are being made more "aware"?

Power. We write books about it. We do not understand it. But understood or not, it is *the issue* as we strive to grow, change, and become different. The masked man and his Indian friend rode into our lives with the issue of power.

Might we be guilty of overstatement? We

think not. Can one resist too much the facades of emotional fascism? Although war is undeclared, there are wounded among us. And these do not hide behind bandages. Nor are they hospitalized. Many of us are suffering great pain from emotional sprains and strains. More are victims of self-expectations. These are the voices crying for help, seeking answers to personal questions, searching for a certainty which will resolve doubt. These are the people who are vulnerable to the Barnums of emotional growth. These are the ones who are not able to see the power issue, and, therefore, are most in need of crap detecting.

To paraphrase, man is infinitely tough and resourceful and not easily cheated of his freedom to be conned. This book will not stop or even slow the con-games of emotional growth. P.T. Barnum was right. However, it is hoped that, at least, you might consider the issues behind the packaging of growth. Furthermore, we have faith that there is an adequate sense of rebellion within. You should be angry when a philosophy, movement, or technique distorts the complexities of a human life with simplicity. You should rebel against emotional come-ons. Today, advantage is being taken.

Finally, this book was written for you and it was written for us. Reinhold Niebuhr, a theologian, first suggested that emancipation requires a commitment outside or beyond the self. As we commit ourselves to your freedom, we are made freer.

We want to be free and powerful, so we wish freedom and power for you.

None of what we have written has been

intended to thwart your desire for assistance, nor is it to suggest there are not some competent people doing some valuable things within the umbrella called emotional growth. It is simply that the Emotional Growth Movement is a vast menage, which allows both wonder and worry to live together. It is up to you to develop your own workable and effective crap detector.

P.S. no more B.S.!

Index